SHATTERED: Touched By Evil

By: Nisaa Corbett

Acknowledgements:

I want to thank the Most High first and foremost. I will always be grateful for every step of my journey. Even in those moments where I thought I would never get back up, he showed me his Mercy and Love.

I would like to THANK my children! They have always been my biggest motivation to move forward. My children think that I am a real life Superwoman and can accomplish ANYTHING, and I love them for that!

I would also like to thank my family. My mother, who I love very much. She taught me that the earth is spacious, and you will never be stuck anywhere where you don't want to be. My father who was always so hard on me but taught me to always keep my eye on the prize and never give up. They both taught me to love God and trust the process.

My brothers and sisters. I love you so much! Ronald, James, Yolanda, Donella, Hassan, Ali, Ibn, and Anas, THANK YOU!

I have so many mentors and friends who helped me along my journey. THANK YOU for your constant support!

The Keeping It Light Team, Brenda McCoy, Gabbi Farrar, and Porscha Anderson! THANK YOU so much for always supporting me.

I would also like to shout out a **HUGE** Thank You to my Editor, **Rochelle Safiyah Ricks!!!!** This woman came to my house everyday with her children after work, went chapter by chapter, and line by line, through my book. She even worked with me, during her lunch breaks. Rochelle, would go through every emotion with me, and never got frustrated or impatient. Words cannot express my gratitude, THANK YOU sis!

Table of Contents

Introduction

It has been reported that Narcissistic Personality Disorder affects at least 6% of the general population. The term Narcissism has been described as the love of self. We all have a bit of Narcissism that helps us maintain a healthy self-image and self-esteem. When we can show love to ourselves, it pushes us in the direction of fulfilling our dreams and goals. The problem arises when Narcissism becomes the leading feature of a person's personality. They begin to develop an inflated sense of self-importance, which makes them believe that others should constantly praise and admire them.

An individual with Narcissistic Personality Disorder, lacks empathy, and does not have the ability to feel any emotion that is not their own. This causes them to latch on to anything that helps them to fill the empty void and darkness, that they feel inside. They have mastered the art of carefully choosing a target, who will give them the most **Narcissistic Supply**. Once the target has been chosen, they use constant manipulation tactics to gain control over them. After some form of control has been gained, they will completely destroy their target emotionally, financially, spiritually, sexually, and the list goes on. A Narcissist can be a male or female. It can also be a family member, friend, boss or co-worker. Also, they do not discriminate when choosing their target. You can be black or white, educated or uneducated, rich or poor, and if they feel like you are an ideal target, your days of happiness and carefree living are numbered.

There are terms related specifically to Narcissistic Personality Disorder, that are used throughout the book. A glossary has been included in the back of the book, just for you!

Chapter 1

Picture your "prince charming," showing up and sweeping you off your feet. He will show you the love, you never thought you would find. He will take away your burdens, making you feel safe and secure. You will share similar goals and dreams. He will call, text, and take you on dates constantly. You are the center of his universe. Well guess what ya'll? I finally met that man. He was so fine, young, and charismatic. Our energy felt magnetic. I was on cloud ten, not nine, but ten. I thought I was in heaven, it felt so good. This man did not miss a beat. I met him at work and after one conversation, we were both hooked.

Let me tell you, it was constant displays of attention everyday all day. He would bring me breakfast in the morning in front of all the women at work, who were trying to pursue him. He would text throughout the day and take me for long walks on our lunch break. We would even go on dates every evening after work. He was spontaneous, always showing me that I was on his mind. I was falling for him, and fast! He made it clear to all the women chasing him, that he had chosen me. I felt like WOW, I had hit the jackpot! You could *not* tell me, I had not been blessed with the man of my dreams. I was on top of the world. After two weeks, he said, "he wanted to make it official, and he wanted me to be in his life forever." He told me I was different from any woman he had ever met. I thought to myself girrrlll, you are BLESSED! Little did I know, I was blessed alright, but not by the Lord. Everything was so rushed. This should have been my sign that something wasn't right. I had never fallen for a man this fast before!

I was so caught up, nose wide open, oblivious to what was really going on. I would later read that this is a textbook manipulation tactic of a Narcissist, called **Love Bombing**. Narcissists use this tactic, so that by the time you figure out something is not right with the relationship, you are too in love to leave. They use constant affection and attention to build a false sense of trust with their targets. Before the target realizes it, all of their defenses are down, and they are in big trouble. The target is sharing their deepest secrets and traumas, which the Narcissist will end up using to destroy them.

The emotional high that you feel with a Narcissist during the love bombing stage, is compared to heavy drugs like cocaine, heroin, and ecstasy. The human brain starts to constantly seek that feeling you've have gotten from the Love Bombing. This constant attention, show of love and romance changes the human brain chemistry and gives it the dopamine rush that it normally gets gradually, in a healthy new relationship. The Narcissist who needs the dopamine rush, just as much as you do, will do everything they can to secure that feeling, because they require what is called **Narcissistic Supply**, to survive and thrive. The problem arises when they can't feel the rush that was there in the beginning, the mask begins to fall off, and the devalue phase starts. The Narcissist has one goal and one goal only for any relationship and that is to **Idealize, Devalue and Discard,** his chosen target. This mind-boggling cycle may be used only one time or many times with the same target over the period of years.

So, a little flashback to my history. Being raised Muslim, it is very important to be married to a Muslim man and to start a family. I tried for many years to find a good match within the guidelines of Islam, but I was unsuccessful in the quest to find my "prince charming." Looking back, I must admit, there were a lot of unresolved issues, that I needed to work on before I would ever have a successful relationship. But honestly, I did not know how to be alone and happy, which made me a prime target for any Narcissist. Even though I had two children, and he was Christian, he let me know he still wanted to move forward with our relationship. Had I listened to my intuition, that was screaming in the background, I would have left this man, six years younger than me, right there in his crib (figuratively).

Against my better judgement, I moved forward anyway. It seemed liked we had been together forever, but I started to realize something just wasn't adding up. I could not put my finger on it. He was still wining and dining me. Spending every free minute, he had available with me. Buying me gifts, doing everything that he started off doing, but my intuition was still screaming at me. Alarms were going off, in every direction. I would walk in on him listening to voicemails left by his ex-girlfriend, crying for him to pick up the phone. He would have a sadistic grin on his face as if he was enjoying listening to her cry. He would tell me to listen to her and how she wanted him back. I recognized that this wasn't normal behavior, but not knowing, this was only the tip of the iceberg.

Once again, I didn't know that this was a typical pattern of a Narcissist. He gets his **Narcissistic supply**, and a twisted satisfaction from hurting others. Narcissistic Supply is attention, approval, adoration, admiration, or anything that the Narcissist uses to stabilize their self-esteem and self-worth, which they themselves lack. They love to think that they won the game of constant manipulation that they play with you. So, even though his ex-girlfriend left the relationship first, she lost the game because she ended up crying to come back for further manipulation. He now viewed her as weak and needing to be punished for not remaining under his control and leaving him. He no longer idealized her as his "prize possession," which started the process known as devalue and discard.

The devalue and discard phase, is designed to break your will, and bring you down to your knees, making you wonder what happened to your "prince charming". You feel worthless, helpless, isolated, and alone, but he has already moved on to his next Narcissistic Supply source. You are no longer of benefit to him and you know who he truly is behind the mask. So, he will walk away like you never existed, but not before he teaches you a lesson. You will be stuck, confused, not knowing what hit you, but guess what, he's not done yet.

He will deploy the next manipulation tactic, known as the **smear campaign**, so that he will appear as the victim and gain the sympathy of his new Narcissistic supply (target) and those around him. A Narcissists main goal for the smear campaign is to discredit and shift responsibility onto the victim and away from themselves. He told me how crazy she was blah blah blah (you know how men say that about every woman they have been with). Of course, I believed him because, I could see his potential beyond his flaws. I had no idea that this is another manipulation

5

tactic used by a Narcissist to further secure his new relationship. He places you on a pedestal, so that you will think you are better than his ex. You will start to do more and more to show him how much better you are than she was. Unwittingly, I fell for his manipulation, and I decided from that moment to just make sure I didn't make the same mistakes she made. I know...I know...LOL...You are reading this probably thinking, "girl you are tripping," and I would have to agree now that I think back.

So, while he is discarding his ex, simultaneously, he is grooming me for the first stages of his narcissistic cycle. During this time, I was unaware of his active manipulation against his ex. In his mind, she has not suffered enough or learned her lesson. He continued to inflict punishment, by idealizing our relationship and showing her how much better I am and showing me how much better I am than her. Now he is at the stage of delivering the **silent treatment**, which allows him to focus solely on our relationship (or so I thought), and completely eliminate her from the picture. He just couldn't get over the fact, that she discarded him, so she will pay. I was feeling sorry for her, little did I know, she was the winner and I was the LOSER. At the same time he is still love bombing me, because he requires as much Narcissistic Supply as possible to make him feel human, to fill that void and emptiness he has inside. If you have had an experience with a

6

Narcissist, you understand that they are always using more than one manipulation tactic to keep you off balance and unsure of your own reality. You will start questioning everything about yourself. All of your insecurities and inadequacies that you ever felt will fall completely out of your closet. These flaws will be fully exposed for the Narcissist to use and exploit for their own twisted benefit.

Chapter 2

Even though everything seemed picture perfect, my focus was still unclear. I just couldn't shake the feeling that something was wrong, even though to everybody around us, I was the luckiest woman in the world. My intuition was screaming at me and I was starting to watch everything around me with a heightened sense of awareness. On one night in particular, I went to sleep, only to be awakened by my "prince charming" under the covers texting someone. I played the part of a trusting girlfriend, and went back to bed, but as soon as he went to sleep, I got up and went in search of his phone (cause I'm nosey as hell). Guess where it was?!?! Behind the toilet! I found message upon message of him berating his ex-girlfriend, saying atrocious things that shocked me. I remember asking myself, "who is this man?"

That next morning when I woke up, I heard the distinctive voice of God telling me to **RUN! RUN AWAY FROM HIM NOW!** I heard the voice, but I did not understand why. I felt like this man was my "prince charming". He made me feel so good. The sense of euphoria I felt with him, I had never felt before. We were already so in tune that we were finishing each other's sentences. I couldn't understand how I was favored in one moment and being ordered to leave my blessing in the next.

I know that sounds crazy, but when you grow up sheltered like I did, the devil knows exactly who and what to send your way. God always spoke to me even as a little girl, but I was what people call "hard-headed." If I didn't understand why you told me not to do something, I went the opposite direction and did it anyway. If only I would have known my disobedience would start a nightmare that would take many, many years to wake up from. I remember in that moment looking back at him and saying to him what God told me. Why I said it to him, I will never understand. He started to cry, not the regular tears but the shoulders-shaking, snot running down your face type of cry.

He said how much he loved me and that he doesn't know why God would tell me to leave. He told me about how his ex and how she had hurt him so bad, and I was helping him to heal. I believed him. In that moment, I made one of the biggest mistakes of my life. I said to myself, I will kick it with him for another two weeks and then let him go. I don't have anything to lose right? WRONG!

Fast forward two weeks later.... I'm sitting in the ob-gyn's office and the doctor tells me I'm pregnant. I just sat there in shock. Although my pregnancy was a blessing, I didn't realize that the next eleven years of my life, would be a repeated cycle of deceit, betrayal and a tangled web of lies that would ultimately bring me down to my knees.

My pregnancy announcement was such a shock to him, it caused his mask to completely fall off. Throwing a monkey wrench in his plan to Idealize, Devalue and Discard me. Spiraling out of control, he started calling me over and over telling me to get an abortion. When that didn't work, he escalated to scare tactics, as a way to force my hand and gain control over the situation. He would tell me that if I didn't get an abortion, he would blow up my uterus and kill the baby himself. He told me that he would make sure that I died, and my body would never be found. He even described the place that he had in mind to dump my body. Fearing for my life, I called a few of my close family and friends who were very discrete. I changed my locks and my phone number. I was scared and confused by his behavior, and also ashamed that I had let the situation get this out of control. I even considered an abortion during that time.

Confused by everything going on in my life, I decided to call my father, who was an Imam or Islamic Leader. I broke down and cried to him about my unplanned pregnancy. He gave me the tough love that I needed in that moment, but he never judged me. I could not bring myself to tell him about the threats made by my so called "prince charming," because I know my father and his temper. I got off the phone and I prayed for guidance. That night I had a vivid dream that I was going to give birth to a beautiful baby girl. I was even able to see her features, skin tone, and curly black hair. After waking up from this dream, I took a deep breath, cried a good cry and started to prepare myself to raise a baby on my own.

So, while dealing with the shame and guilt of getting pregnant out of wedlock, I was dealing with a crazy dude that I thought was "prince charming," but he was really a wolf in sheep's clothing. My mind was made up though, I had just gotten out of a bad relationship, so I wasn't settling for the nonsense that he was dishing out. I was finally on my own, new city (Houston), new job making great money, new apartment, new furniture, new life and soon I would have a new baby. I started to feel like I could this. I was going on with my life, by any means necessary

Chapter 3

You thought the story was over, didn't you? LOL...Me Too

Although this story should be over, a Narcissist will never let you get away that easy. The love bombing, and **Hoovering** starts all over again. He begged for forgiveness. He cried saying he wanted to be a part of his child's life, and we would get married "eventually". He knew this would get me because of how important my religion was to me. He figured out with me being embarrassed and ashamed about my pregnancy, I would abandon being around people. I just wanted to hide. I know this sounds crazy, but I grew up in a very strict Muslim household, so this was instilled in me. I decided after a couple of weeks to give him another chance, because I didn't want my child to be fatherless. Little did I know, I was in for the ride of my life. Remember I told you, I always have to learn my lessons the hard way. This decision would almost kill me in more ways than one.

Fast forward, a couple of days later. He asked me to start all over, and forget "his" past mistakes. My "prince charming" moved in with me. Did I tell him that he could; no, he just came over and never left. Every day I would find a new item that belonged to him in my house. This is a perfect example of how a Narcissist will test your boundaries to see how far they can go in the beginning. He quickly moved in and did not respect anything that I had in place. If I asked him not to wear his shoes in the house, he wore his shoes anyway and told me how stupid the rule was. If I told him not to bring pork in the house because of religious reasons and the fact that my children sometimes cannot decipher whether something is pork or not, he would bring it into the house anyway and put it right into the refrigerator.

I would argue, but after a while I just ignored his lack of respect, just to keep the peace around my boys. I was already having issues with my pregnancy, so I kept my focus on taking care of my unborn baby and my children. My doctor told me that my pregnancy may end in a miscarriage due to all the health issues I was experiencing. I was also working full-time, so life was very hectic, and I was honestly scared. I didn't want to lose my baby.

We decided with me being pregnant and needing more space, moving to a bigger place would make sense. The move was great, it felt like a fresh start for my new family. I was excited. It started off wonderful. We had a beautiful place. I was working, he was going to school and working. He would come home in the evening, cook dinner and even bring me my plate. I'm not talking small meals, but he would go all out every night! He would clean the house and do the laundry all without me asking. I mean wash, dry, fold, AND put away the laundry! I had never had a man do these things for me before. Too good to be true right?!?!?

The games eventually started, the disappearing acts, late nights at the gym, new phone numbers from women in his phone. He would even go as far as hiding his phone at night or even if he was home in the daytime. My intuition is screaming at me, but I guess I wasn't ready to accept that my "prince charming" never really existed. He ended up having to end his employment, because his school schedule was so intense. Although, he never included me in the decision; I understood why he had to do it.

He was still getting money from family members and also student loans, so I didn't mind. The problem came in when I told him I needed help paying for a couple of things for the baby, and he looked me dead in my face and said: "Since you decided to have the baby, you can figure out how to pay everything pertaining to the baby on your own." He knew I was struggling, trying to work and stay afloat. I was still having major problems with my pregnancy. I couldn't believe his lack of empathy and I guess I just didn't understand it. I just assumed it was due to his age and lack of maturity. Eventually his money stopped coming in, and I ended up paying most of the bills.

My situation was getting out of control! I have always been independent and taken care of my business, but now I had somebody who is dead weight and adding to my struggle. More strange behaviors started to get my attention. I started having nightmares about him. He would not let me meet his friends or spend time with his friends. The only person I had access to, was his best friend, and that was only because they lived together. Everything was a secret. I never spoke to his mother directly until I was about to deliver my baby. He would say his family knew all about me, but after I had my baby his father explained that they never knew I was I pregnant until the very end.

I figured out later that a Narcissist likes to keep you separate from their friends and family. It is easier to manipulate the situation, if the people they are playing against each other don't speak. They can easily spin stories and will always come out as a victim, gaining the sympathy and the attention that they need for Narcissistic supply. This also helps them to gain supporters, who have not heard your side of the story, so they assume it's the truth. These supporters will eventually become "**flying monkeys**" for the Narcissist and will be recruited to assist with the smear campaign to destroy your reputation and further abuse you. This manipulation tactic called **Triangulation**, is often used by Narcissists, usually enlisting friends, colleagues, family members, coworkers, neighbors, and anybody that will listen to their victimhood and sympathize with them. They will even record you secretly during arguments, so they can send the recordings to their supporters as proof that YOU are crazy. So, while you are arguing, they are sitting back cool, calm, and collected knowing that you are being recorded.

All of this is to teach you a lesson, because they are slowly losing the control that they once had over you. The Narcissist will do ANYTHING to regain that control. They will always use a third party against you, who will side with them. Based solely on the stories told by the Narcissist. The end goal is to ensure no one believes your story about the abuse and you will be labeled a liar. Ironically, they really don't want you to leave, after all you are a great source of Narcissistic supply. Imagine this being your life? Your reality with a man who you fell head over heels for, you have planned your future with, and he is the father of your unborn child? Hold that thought.

You have to remember that the Narcissist works in cycles, which can be continuous. At the end of one cycle, the honeymoon phase starts over, and the Narcissist will work hard to regain your trust. The Narcissist will make you believe you are the most important person in their lives. The gifts will start, expensive trips, with promises of a brighter future. Nobody can Love Bomb like a Narcissist. The Narcissist is not smarter than you, just prepared. They are always one step ahead because they have planned everything from the moment you became their target. You are operating out of a place of love, the same thing that they view as a weakness. They are operating from a place of selfishness, anger, depression, jealousy, and darkness. The Narcissist has studied and learned your strengths, but what is most important and useful to them is your weaknesses.

Chapter 4

Case and point, while running errands one day, I ran into a good friend of his and she revealed all the lies he was spreading about me. All the while we were living together. He discussed my "flaws" with her, subjects that we had discussed during pillow talk. He told her that I was crazy and on various medications. She even recognized that this was not normal behavior and felt that she needed to let me know. I was shocked and devastated. I realized he was not only a manipulative man but a pathological liar who had zero regard for me. Clueless, I was the last to know, even his family admitted that he was a liar and had been since childhood. They also revealed that he had been abusive to women prior to our relationship (more red flags).

As time moved on, I was starting to become more depressed and anxious. A shell of myself. He was constantly making me question my own reality. I would clearly see text messages that he would tell me I didn't see or I misread them. If I said the sky was blue, he would say it was green. This is a slow methodical process called **Gaslighting**. Narcissists use this tactic, to make you start questioning your reality. They start to do things that will make you feel paranoid, overly sensitive, silly, and mentally unstable. Once they notice this tactic is working they will start the finger pointing and shifting the blame for every negative event onto you. Some examples of things he would say frequently during our relationship: "stop being so sensitive," or "you are overreacting," or "you are becoming obsessed," or "you are not normal."

Narcissists will start to minimize how you feel by asking questions like, "why are you being so sensitive?", "why are you getting angry over something so small?" During this time, you will start to feel like you are losing it, and you stop speaking up for yourself. Eventually you start to feel powerless and less confident. Doubting yourself, and apologizing for everything, because maybe you are too sensitive. The woman who was once confident and ready to take on the world becomes a shell of her former self. Gaslighting throws you off emotionally and causes you to doubt your perceptions and memories. You will start to rely more on the Narcissist because you no longer trust your judgements and perceptions. This is how a Narcissist grooms you to stay with them, even when you know better. You begin to think you need them and can't make it without them. You are slowly being erased.

At this point, he started working again. He was maintaining a hectic work and school schedule. I tried to be an understanding partner, despite of red flags. I knew he was with other women, so I would just search and search for clues, while he was constantly feeding me lies about the kind of man he was pretending to be. I would look at our phone bill and would see at times where he was supposed to be unavailable, he was texting and calling other women. I would find messages to his ex-girlfriend, which he would claim only happened because he had been drinking. I was slowly losing myself and my grip on reality. My anxiety was at an all-time high. We were fighting constantly. Now, don't get me wrong, I was no angel. He wasn't going to keep playing me, and I would often let him know that.

Friends and coworkers were asking me what was wrong, because I looked tired, stressed and had lost a ton of weight. My best friend would say, "this crap ain't normal." I even had a close male coworker who would tell me that I was in an abusive relationship, and that something was really wrong with the man I was dating. He pointed out, "prince charming's" abnormal family dynamic and that I needed to open my eyes. Looking back, boy was he right on point.

Typically, a Narcissist has grown up with a Narcissistic parent in the household. Now that I understand what Narcissism is and how a Narcissistic mother interacts with her child, I see exactly the misery that my "prince charming", endured as a child. I wish I would have had more of an opportunity to speak with his mother at the beginning of the relationship, so maybe I would have picked-up on the unhealthy dynamic, but he would not let me speak to her. Honestly, it probably wouldn't have changed anything because bottom line is, I'm an Empath and a fixer. The combination of both made me a dream target for a Narcissist.

During this time, I realized I was no longer functioning at full capacity. I couldn't think outside of my relationship, it was consuming my whole life. If he felt like my attention was going elsewhere, he would find a way to regain my full attention, whether it was positive or negative. I couldn't even focus on my children without him getting angry and punishing me. Narcissists often get jealous and compete with anybody, who takes attention away from them, even their own children.

Slowly, he is gaining more control. He started to play next level mind games. He would purposefully leave ex-girlfriends pictures up on the monitor knowing I would see them. Even going as far as searching websites for paternity testing options for our unborn child and leaving them up to provoke a negative reaction. He also started openly contacting females on social media and leaving it in plain view, so I could see it. My "prince charming," started coming home later than usual without any explanation, at times I couldn't reach him at all during the day. Changing his routine, kept me off balance and in a constant state confusion. When I asked him about his disappearing acts, he had an excuse for everything. He even started hanging out with random male friends and would get defensive if I asked any questions about them. My internal voice is screaming that something is seriously wrong, but I was completely stomped. I could feel darkness in my soul. I couldn't rest. I knew if I didn't get it together soon or figure it out, I was going to lose it.

Chapter 5

The internal turmoil caused me to pray more and more for guidance. God hadn't left me though even in my disobedience, he led me exactly to what I was dealing with. One day I typed some of his behaviors in the Google search engine and the word Narcissism popped up. Once I started reading about it, I knew I had found my life line. There was an actual name for what I was dealing with and I wasn't crazy. I couldn't believe that someone that close could possess such evil qualities, and I was sleeping with him. Maybe, I was wrong? Maybe, I was just overreacting? What about all of the good times that we shared? I could not accept the reality that I was with a soulless man, who lacked empathy and was incapable of loving ANYBODY but himself.

He had no boundaries, he was above all of the rules that regular human beings followed, they did not apply to him. So many things became clear to me. I would scream at him during arguments about his superiority complex and lack of boundaries. Even with this information right in front of me I couldn't just leave, my daughter needed her father. He always told me that if we broke up, he would move back to Georgia with his family. In spite of his character flaws, I still wanted to be married, so that I could right my wrongs. I lived with this man and had gotten pregnant - how would I be forgiven if I didn't get married? Now that my faith is stronger, I know how crazy that sounds, but hey we all live, and we learn. While I was trying to figure out how to fix my relationship, so many things were going on behind the scenes that I didn't know about, but it would all soon come to the forefront. What is done in the dark always comes to the light.

One afternoon, He left his email open by "accident," and I saw that once again he was communicating with his ex-girlfriend. Curious, I contacted her, and she reached out to me. She told me that he asked her to get back together and to get married. I informed her that he was still living with me, and I was pregnant. She verified my story and confronted him. After speaking with him, it was confirmed that all of this was a part of sick twisted plan of revenge to pay her back for discarding him. I was shocked!

He wanted her to make plans, tell her family and friends so that he could embarrass and discard her publicly. She shared other disturbing things that she endured during their relationship. She recalled an argument when he took her feet and dragged them through glass that was on the floor. I didn't believe her, so I asked him. He admitted to doing it and in turn told me how good it felt to hear her cry out in pain knowing she was hurting the same way she had hurt him during their relationship.

I cannot explain the things that went through my mind during this time. I knew I needed to get away, but I just couldn't believe that a human being could be so evil. My breaking point, was the day I found more emails from her, I decided that I couldn't take it anymore. I called him to end our relationship, and to let him know his stuff will be packed and on the front porch. I changed the locks and taped all the emails that I found to the outside of the door for him to see.

This would be the first time that I saw the demon within my "prince charming." I had opened Pandora's Box, unleashing the dragon. He came home and BOOM, kicked the door down. His strength that day was super natural. I'm not talking a little off the hinges, but completely off the hinges. The metal frame was destroyed. My kids are screaming from the room. I moved towards the back of the apartment, as he comes through the front door. He runs after me and starts to choke me until I lost my breath. This would be the first of many times that he would wrap his hands around my neck. He knocked me into the wall and told me he would kill me. He told me that I didn't know who I was dealing with. I tried to fight back but this is man is an avid weight lifter. He eventually let go of me and walked out. He went to stay with his brother. Little did I know he would stay there because he and his step-niece, were engaging in inappropriate behaviors. That's a whole other "can of worms." SMH.

That night my kids and I stayed in the house, with no front door. I just leaned the door up against the door frame and put my children to bed. I stayed up that whole night, just crying. How could I be in this place? I am a fighter. I am a strong woman. I was so disappointed in myself. The funny thing about a Narcissist, is they don't discriminate whether you are strong or weak, black or white, rich or poor, educated or uneducated, Muslim or Christian, you can get it too! I was so scared laying in that house with no door, but he didn't care because he said I made him mad and I deserved it. This is normal behavior for a Narcissist because they lack empathy, caring less about your feelings or safety.

A couple of days later after the silent treatment my "prince charming" resurfaced. He called me with the victim role that he

24

always played so well, and I fell once again hook, line, and sinker. He explained to me that he didn't want a relationship with his ex-girlfriend, and how he just wanted to teach her a lesson. He started to cry and promise that he just wants to be a great father and "future husband." Which he couldn't do be because I would not trust him. Me, trust issues, Really?!?!? This is the same person who disappears during the day and night, lies about his school and work schedule, hides his phone, texts and calls other women. Bottom line is, the Narcissist will ALWAYS be the victim in any situation.

Love will sometimes make you look like a stone cold fool. Little did I know, he had already set the trap. I loved the fact that he knew so much about me, but after researching the traits of a Narcissist, anything they know about you, especially weaknesses, can and will be used to manipulate or destroy you. You are usually totally blind to the fact that they are already destroying your reputation to family and friends, so when you finally realize what's going on and you try to expose them, you are already considered the "crazy one". The Narcissist has already made sure everybody knows you are "mentally unstable." They are strategic planners, who try to cover most of their bases. When they realize you can no longer be controlled, they attempt to control the way others see you.

Chapter 6

As time progressed, I was starting to lose myself more and more. I wanted to do anything to make my relationship work, but it was becoming damn near impossible. I ended up having to go on bed rest because my daughter had her own plans and wanted to come early due to the Hurricane. I went into preterm labor at about 27 weeks. My "prince charming" was there with me the whole time. He catered to my every need, and only left my side to get my kids from his brother's house. I thought once again we were on track, but with a narcissist their love is not real.

It's all a facade, a show that they put on for attention. The minute we arrived back home, I found a text message from him to another woman saying that he wanted to, "take her from the back." This is a slang term used for having sex with a woman from behind. He argued that I didn't read what I thought I read and that I misinterpreted the message. I was devastated. I felt physically sick to my stomach. I just couldn't understand how he could smile in my face and be so attentive yet do those things behind my back. The stress was becoming too much, and I was beginning to have frequent and more painful contractions. I gave him hell about it, but we ultimately pushed it to the side for the sake of our unborn child. I put the blinders on once again. I was quiet for the moment, but being a detective by nature, I was going to find out about everything. And I mean **EVERYTHING**.

Although the hospital was able to stop my contractions, I still ended up on bed rest for the remainder of my pregnancy. I had to stop working during this time, which gave me a lot more time to pay attention to my surroundings. I had to give myself terbutaline shots twice a day, to stop my body from going into labor. I was also hooked up to a monitor, so that nurses could watch my contractions remotely throughout the day. I was having contractions sometimes five minutes apart every day, all day. It was terrible. Morning sickness became my best friend, so I was sick day after day. Not only in the morning, but all day. I threw up so much I had to have a trash can beside my bed. My depression during this time was unbearable, but do you think that stops the Narcissist?

Not at all. A Narcissist likes to kick you when you're down, this is another way for them to secure their supply. During this time, He would constantly tell me that I wasn't showing him enough attention. He would stay out later than usual and ignore my calls throughout the day. Disregarding medical advice, he wanted to have sex with me and would scream at me if I didn't go along. The doctors had already told us that sexual activity could cause the baby to come early, so I was trying to be very careful since I know the dangers of having a baby prematurely.

Eventually he started going to his brother's house for "sleepovers", where he couldn't be reached after a certain hour. If I wouldn't have been pregnant I would have played Magnum PI, but my baby was more important than his mind games at that time. I started to realize his selfishness. It was all about him and his wants and needs. Him wanting 24-hour attention, admiration and porn star skills all wrapped up in one person. Imagine that.

While I was on bedrest, his best friend and girlfriend would occasionally come over and eat and spend time with me. He and his best friend were so close, that everybody called them cousins. He was really the only friend of "prince charming's," that I had access to from the beginning. One day while visiting, his best friends tone turned serious, he looked at me said "you are a really good woman." I replied, a little confused because he looked concerned. Nevertheless, I thanked him. He then said, "he is not who you think he is, and once you get to know him you are not going to like him." I was taken aback in that moment, but it really made me think about my current situation. The fact that these two men were so close, but his best friend felt like he needed to tell me that. He also told me about my "prince charming," and his frequent drug use when visiting his brother's house. I was shocked! I wish I would have questioned him more, but tragically he was murdered days later. My whole world was spinning out of control after his death. I kept replaying what he told me in my mind. My intuition was also screaming at me. After his friend died he cried only one time. He showed no interest in trying to find out who murdered him. He was emotionless and showed a lack of concern, which gave me an uneasy feeling. I know everybody grieves differently, but it caught my attention. How could someone's best friend move all the way to Houston to be close, and his unsolved murder does not affect you. Even my young children questioned his behavior.

I started having more vivid nightmares about my situation. The one that I remember most is the one where my "prince charming" was a King Cobra snake. I dreamed, all my children were in different parts of the house, and I was trying to get them out one by one. He would strike out with each child I grabbed. I was able to get them all out, but this dream scared me. I was told that dreams about snakes mean somebody that you are close to may be your enemy. I started to watch him more closely, what jumped out the most to me was all of a sudden, he wanted bizarre sexual positions. He never asked for specific type of positions, so I was definitely on high alert. He was also disappearing again. I found receipts from him hanging out at bars and lounges during his school hours. When I would ask him had he been there, he would lie. He looked me straight in my eyes and told me he was not at the place that was on the receipt. There would be receipts with drinks on them that he would never order, so I knew he wasn't alone.

I just couldn't understand how someone could lie without batting an eye; it was almost like he believed his own lies. I had never met anyone like him before. So cool and confident, even as he lies. My eyes were wide open at this point. I became super vigilant about things that were going on around me. I became paranoid. I stepped up my game, checking emails, phones, etc., my life was completely out of control at this point. I became obsessed with figuring it all out.

One day, I found something on my private area that was not supposed to be there. I went to the doctor and they told me, I had genital warts or HPV. My mouth completely dropped open. I had never had a Sexually Transmitted Infection in my entire life. I'm pregnant, going through preterm labor and now my baby has been exposed to a STI. I was livid! I went to him and of course he blamed it on me and said that I had been cheating. Anything he

30

could come up with to get the attention away from him. I think I was more in shock at that moment and I was also in fear for my baby. The doctors had explained that it was an infection my baby could contract going through my birth canal. I drove home in a daze. From the moment I got home, I would just sit in my house and cry, because this was something that could potentially hurt my innocent baby.

Do you think he showed any concern? No, not at all. I went alone to the hospital for the procedure. I ended up having laser surgery to remove the warts. I was so scared and confused, but I was able to get through it. I remember laying on the cold table, with only the doctor there to comfort me. I couldn't tell anybody, because I was embarrassed and ashamed. The surgery was so painful. I even cry as I write this. The experience was so humiliating. By the grace of God I have had no symptoms since that day and I test negative for the virus that causes genital warts and leads to ovarian cancer.

He refused to go to the doctor and get checked. I thought back to the text that I found earlier of him saying he wanted to take the girl from the back, and I contacted her. The girl responded right away and told me that she also had an outbreak of genital warts and that they had been sexually active at some point. She also tried to calm my fears by telling me that the body can sometimes naturally heal itself from HPV. I was so outdone. Here I am 8 months pregnant and my life is in absolute shambles. Little did I know he had went and told family and friends about my STI and told them that I had been unfaithful to him. I didn't find this information out until the end of our relationship, so imagine my shock. Once again, he framed himself as a victim. I felt so violated all the way around. I would just sit in my room and pray for me and my children and the strength to do what I obviously needed to do. God always guided me and gave me my answers.

You probably thought this was the end of my story, but we are not even close.

Why did I stay even when all the signs were there? At this time, all my friends didn't even know I was pregnant because I was unmarried. I wasn't talking to my family as much because I felt like I was in a bad situation. I was embarrassed about my circumstances and I wanted to hide the truth as much as possible. Little did I know, I was right where the Narcissist wanted me to be. Feeling ALONE and isolated. Remember, I was on bed rest and could not leave my house during this time. My mind started going a mile a minute. I started to think about my unresolved issues from childhood, and my failed relationships. I began to think maybe I was the problem? He had sniffed out all of my "flaws" and imperfections like a blood hound. He saw my need for love, validation, and affection, and exploited my fear of abandonment.

The Narcissist studies his target carefully. Determining exactly who you need in a mate and mirroring those exact traits. My "prince charming," had studied my relationship with my children. He knew that I loved hard. He would watch me with my kids and how much I nurtured and loved them. At first, he admired that connection I have with my children, but it became a competition later. He went so far as to accuse me of having sex with my oldest son, because we were so close. He would also say things like you love your children more that you love me. If I went to spend time in their room like I used to do before we got together, he would get enraged and punish me with the infamous silent treatment or an argument where he would leave the house.

Chapter 7

Finally, the time had arrived, to give birth to our baby girl. Lo and Behold, the pains kicked in on "prince charming's," birthday. I thought this would be such a blessing for him on his special day. I was so excited to call and tell him the news! His reaction was not what I expected at all. He got very upset and shouted that this was his day, and he didn't want her born on his birthday. He asked me if I could lie down, while he went out and hung out for his birthday, to prevent my labor from progressing. I did exactly that. The disappointment and hurt that I felt in that moment was unbearable. I could not understand how someone could be this selfish, but my priority at that moment was my child.

I ended up giving birth the next morning. We went to the hospital and about an hour later my baby was born. I was so in love from the moment I saw her. She was his twin. It was like he had her all on his own. This was his first time watching a birth although he has another child from a previous relationship. That situation is a whole other set of lies, but that is for another book. He was in awe of our baby girl. In my heart I felt like this was the moment our life would change, and it did, for a very short time. After we took baby girl home he was a very attentive father. He fed her, changed her, clothed her. I felt like everything I had been through was worth it for her to experience that type of love from him. I'm the type of mother who will do anything to ensure my children have a good life, even if it means I have to sacrifice myself. That's exactly what I did.

Everything was great until he started exhibiting behaviors that didn't make sense once again. If she cried he thought it was okay to put her in the bathroom or closet with the light off and close the door. We would argue about it. He didn't seem to do it in a malicious manner, but he did not understand why it was not okay. My son and I would simply go and get her each time. It didn't make sense before but now that I understand a Narcissist not being able to feel basic human emotions, I can understand the behavior.

The mind games started once again, because my attention was more towards our baby than him. I found a text where he was talking to a close friend of his, and she was explaining how she wished she would have made the move on him before he got with me. Of course, according to him "I didn't really see the text," or "I must have misread the text." I would also see text where his sister would try to reach out and get to know me and he would say we didn't need to know each other and would delete her messages to him.

Trying to make it work, I was convinced to move to a nicer place not far from our apartment, so that we would have more space. I really didn't want to get anything that cost more than we were paying because I knew how volatile our relationship was. I ended up going back to my job after my maternity leave ended and we moved. Shortly after that I decided that I should enroll in community college, which was located right across the street. I was making good money at my job, but I knew I was capable of making way more with my skill set and a degree would only enhance that. The move was great for a while. Our place was gorgeous, and I felt happy.

We started taking trips and enjoying each other. He bought me a "promise ring", saying that we were going to get married soon. We even took a trip to see his family in Georgia, so that they could meet our baby girl. It was my first time meeting them. I noticed that their interaction as a family was very strange. I was told by people very close to them stories about their "weird" family dynamic. I was also told that the mother never allowed anyone to get close to her son, and that she would do ANYTHING to get the other party out of the picture. I was even told that she practices witchcraft, but I did not believe it at first. I heard the warnings, but I wanted to give them the benefit of the doubt since I had never been around them.

I quickly learned that they were not people that I could trust. The mother had already started spreading lies about me and telling people I was taking advantage of her son and keeping him from being successful. She told people that I had messed up his graduation date and now he would be graduating later than scheduled. She had no idea that when I met her son, he was just enrolling in school and had not attended all that time prior to me coming into the picture. He had been lying telling his family that he was in school. Also, I found out he was doing drugs all that time, even when he met me. When I confronted him about it he claims that he had eventually stopped before our baby was born, but I don't think I will ever really know the truth.

I decided eventually to leave my job and concentrate on school exclusively. I was in a place financially where I could do so and it would not interfere with what I already had going on. It was quiet for a short time after that, but eventually all of the mind games continued. He started disappearing again, new numbers started popping up in his cell phone. One day when he didn't come home and would not respond to my messages, I logged into his account

I found that he was at a restaurant not far from my house. The amount spent was obviously for more than one person, so I got up, dressed and went to the restaurant. He was sitting there with another woman and when I approached them, would not say anything. When she realized who I was and what was going on, she said "it's not what you think." She also looked at him and asked, "why he wasn't saying anything," because she didn't want any drama. He had this sick twisted smirk on his face the whole time as if he enjoyed the whole interaction. The infamous **Narcissistic Smirk**. He eventually ran off into his car and left, but she and I stayed and had a long conversation.

She was very apologetic and swore to me that they were only friends. She revealed to me that they would meet-up to discuss her relationship issues, because her boyfriend was abusive. I explained to her, that he was the wrong person to get advice from, because he is also abusive. She told me how he said that I was crazy and on all types of medications. She also told me about all of the other things he was saying about me as well. I was no longer surprised or shocked about the things he would say. She was surprised that I was not the person he described and wanted to keep in touch. We ended up exchanging numbers and I went home.

When I got home he was in the bed. I attempted to get undressed and get into the bed as well. We did not speak in that moment, but every time I would try to get on the bed, he would physically kick me off. After many attempts, I stopped trying to get on the bed and we started arguing. I was screaming and cussing about the things that were said about me to the female. Out of the blue, he grabbed me and slammed me onto the bed. In the middle of this, I am calling a male friend of mine that lives in the complex, but he knocks the phone out of my hand. He put his arms around my whole body in a bear hug, lays on top of me with his full body weight and squeezes me so hard that I cannot breathe. I am kicking, letting out any sound that I can. In that moment I thought I was going to die. Nobody could hear me. All I could think of was my kids being asleep in the other room. If I die who would take care of them? Would they find my body? He finally released me and rolled over in the bed to sleep as if nothing ever happened. I just laid there in shock, with tears streaming down my face. I couldn't process what had just happened to me. The evil look that he had in his face and the darkness in his eyes just kept replaying in my mind.

The next day my friend called back because when he woke up and checked his messages, he could hear me screaming for my "prince charming" to let me go and get off me. When the phone fell, and he didn't answer, the call went to his voicemail and he could hear everything. My friend was so scared and angry. I told him that I was fine, and we left it at that. We were so close, that he knew not to push the issue.

Not long after that incident, I received a message from his ex-girlfriend. Once again, he was reaching out to her, so she was reaching out to me. We talked about the abuse she encountered with him. How he used to choke her etc. She talked about how she felt like she was in a web that she could not escape. I told her to look up Narcissism and she was shocked once she read the first few lines. She told me that all of the characteristics of Narcissism was what she went through with him. After this we formed a bond, that stayed intact over the years. I also reached out to the mother of his child and she admitted that she went through the same type of things we went through including the physical abuse. We also formed a bond and an understanding. He had started his abusive pattern at a very young age. He had moved to Houston because of his abuse towards the mother of his child. He quickly got into another relationship when he moved to Houston which lasted two years, and shortly after that I came along.

Chapter 8

During this time, I ended up in the hospital. I had a complete nervous breakdown. Although I was still in school, taking care of my babies and trying to act like everything was okay, it was all getting to be too much for me to handle. I cracked under the pressure. My therapist was telling me that I needed to look at my relationship. He explained that my "prince charming" should be the one in the hospital, and not me. I was still hiding the complete truth from mostly everybody, even the doctors. I would give them bits and pieces of information, but never the brutal truth of my situation. He would come and eat with me during my hospital stay. I noticed that he was in some of his happiest moods while I was in and out of the hospital. That made me think even further, that it was me bringing him down, not knowing, he could not and would NEVER be able to feel my pain.

I started to think back to my previous relationships that did not work and considered that maybe the problem was me. Every time we would get in an argument, and I would tell him about the things he was doing, he would accuse me of those same behaviors. It was always like arguing with a brick wall. We never got anywhere, and it was so exhausting. I started trying to work on my issues, that I had from childhood, thinking that maybe I was doing something to make him so angry. It got so bad that my family came from different states to rally around me and to figure out what was wrong. They only knew me as the strong, independent woman. They didn't know the woman that was sitting in front of them broken and not wanting to go on. My family didn't know the reality of my situation. I couldn't stop crying. Once again, I turned to the Most High for strength and guidance.

I finally was able to find the strength to move forward. I got up and kept fighting. The situation in my house improved briefly. He would always take me on surprise trips, shopping, or to nice restaurants and treat me like a queen following the abuse. We would even go as a family, and it made me think, if I could only hang in there and continue to love him that everything would be okay. This idea created a bit of **cognitive dissonance**, because although I knew the truth about who he really was, my mind went to all of the good times that we shared at the beginning. I always thought that we could get back to that place, not fully understanding that it was not real. I was a carefully chosen target. His plan was to idealize, devalue and eventually discard me, but I got pregnant.

My children truly kept me going from day to day. My daughter was growing up, my sons were doing well despite of the situation. I tried to hide the reality of the situation from them as much as possible. I was lucky that my boys both had their fathers in their lives, so they were able to see positive male role models who taught them how to be real men. I truly thank God for his mercy.

Shortly after getting back on track all the games began again. He started hanging out with co-workers, and when I would even ask their names he would get defensive. He became even more secretive than he was before. I was starting to get more and more fed up. We would fight and argue about it, but it only got worse. I remember reading messages between he and his sister and he was telling her how I was being abusive to him and trying to break him down. She replied that "I was crazy and for him to be strong." I couldn't believe my eyes. He was telling people that I was the abuser. Really?!?!

One night, he went to hang out with one of his male co-workers and did not come home until 8:00 in the morning. I tried to reach him, but his phone was off. From that point, I was like Hell No! When he arrived home that morning, I found a message in his cell phone from that night, and he was talking to a female from his past again. He explained that he got drunk that night and passed out until that morning. Of course, I did not believe him. After this incident, I started to become very angry, and hostile towards him. I knew the day would come when we would soon part.

Everything changed one day, when I walked into the bedroom and saw him looking intently out the window. I stood and just watched him for a moment, and a strange feeling came over me. I got chills all over my body. I went over to the window and there were two young black men making out in front of the pool. I looked over at him and the look on his face made me sick to my stomach.

43

I just sat there and stared at him. In that moment, I remembered something his ex-girlfriend and the mother of his child had told me previously. Immediately, he became angry and agitated. He started pushing me until he pushed me against a wall. He told me I didn't see anything, and he threatened to hurt me.

I knew at that point he had to go. I don't know what I saw, but after that incident everything went downhill. I ended up putting him out of my house. We argued, and I threw some of his things over the balcony. He later brought the police to the house telling them that I didn't give him his things. I let him in to get the rest of his stuff and the police asked me if they could talk to me. They asked me a little about the situation and I told them why I would not let him back in. I let them know that he likes to get physical with me and I wasn't going to deal with it anymore. Once he left they looked at me and told me you need to rid yourself of that situation. They commented that although they don't know him, they can see that I needed to move forward, especially for my children. After he left, I didn't hear from him for the rest of the day.

Eventually, he resurfaced. He sent me an email begging me to contact him. He would call over and over again. He used every Hoover tactic in the Narcissist manual. He sent many emails making himself into the victim. He talked about what kind of person I was for putting him out with no family in town. He would call me sobbing saying, "he thought I loved him, and we were soul mates who were meant for each other." Also, he would say, "he wanted to get married sooner than later." He even lied and said that he had been sleeping in his car. I finally contacted his father and mother and let them know about the physical abuse that I had been experiencing over the years. His dad commented that he was not surprised and that if it happened again to send him to jail. He specifically told me that he would not bail his son out, because obviously he had not learned his lesson from previous incidents with ex-girlfriends. His mom blamed me but admitted that he had done it to other women in the past.

I held my ground and did not let him come back. I remained in school during this time, and that's where I put a lot of my energy. I even started talking to another gentleman in attempts to move forward. It felt good to finally be moving on. I decided to move to a different apartment which was cheaper, so that I could handle all the bills on my own with no problem. I couldn't really depend on child support from him because he would send it to my bank account and cancel the payment if I did not agree to meet up with him. It was hard financially, but God always provided for me and my children.

My children once again kept me going. They were happy about the new start. He would come pick up our daughter periodically, which was fine with me. One morning he called crying and said that he needed to talk to me to apologize for everything that had transpired. I listened, because I still had unresolved feelings for him. He wanted to come by even though it was 2:00 in the morning, so you know that conversation turned into something totally different. After we had sex, it was like we fell back into the same old destructive pattern.

Approximately, a month later, while I was visiting my parents' house, my step-dad commented on my weight gain. I had not noticed with everything that had been going on. Lo and behold, a week later I found out I was pregnant with my fourth child. I was shocked and devastated. How the hell was I going to take care of another child by myself. As soon as I told him, he went and told everybody that I trapped him. He said that I had stopped taking my birth control; just blatant lies. His mother called me and told me to get an abortion because her son cannot take care of anymore children. I politely informed her that her son took sex education just like I did, and I got her off my phone.

At this point, our relationship was pretty much touch and go. I took care of everything with my children and continued going to school. Many days I just wanted to give up, but I had close friends who kept reminding me about how my degree would not only change my life but the lives of my children. This alone just made me push so much harder. Depression and anxiety became my best friends, but I kept pushing through. I started taking more online classes. My older son would hold down the fort while I studied, took test etc. He was always my rock, especially during this time.

I struggled to get everything I needed for my new addition. He would not help me with anything, so during this time I depended a lot on friends and family. I remember one day, he called me so excited, and told me he had a surprise for me and that I was going to be happy. When he arrived I just knew he had purchased an item for our child since he had not helped me at all during my pregnancy and it was almost time for me to give birth. Guess what it was?? It was a brand-new car that he had purchased for himself. Yes, I said for HIMSELF! When I saw the car, the wind was knocked out of me. Initially, he had told me he would buy an SUV , so that everybody could fit into the car when we travel. He was so happy about his new purchase and could not understand why I was not. I was so outdone. I didn't even have a car seat to put in the car at that moment. SMH

Chapter 9

During this time in my pregnancy, we used to go to each other's houses for sleepovers, so he could help with our daughter. One day I went over, and we got into an argument about where he had been the night before. Catching me off guard, he punched me in the side of my pregnant belly. I fell to the floor crying and in pain. He responded by telling me that he never touched me and that I was lying. I ran out of the house to call the police. He then runs after me and breaks my phone in half and threatens to hurt me further if I contact the police. After this incident I kept my distance for a long while. He would still get my daughter but sometimes would say he was going to get her and never show up.

One night he kept dodging my calls when he was supposed to pick her up, so I called and let him know that I was coming, and I went to his house. He opens the door and I place my daughter inside of the door with him. He slams the door and I ran down the stairs to my car. I received a call the following day saying that a neighbor had found my child roaming around outside all by herself. They told me that an officer had figured out which door to knock on and her father was given a citation. They were conducting an investigation, and I had to tell them the events that took place that evening. He was eventually found responsible for allowing my two-year-old daughter to roam outside without adult supervision. He never showed any remorse for this incident, and never returned calls to Child Protective Services regarding the incident. Remember, rules do not apply to a Narcissist. They don't have to answer to anyone.

I could not for the life of me understand why I could not stay away from this man. It was like I was a drug addict and he was my drug. My gut told me to stay away but my heart always took over. I didn't know that all of the constant ups and downs were part of the process that a Narcissist uses called **trauma bonding**. It is a form of domination used by an abuser where you are constantly experiencing pleasure and pain through their actions, so you become addicted to the feeling. It also gives them a feeling of power and control over you, as well as a view into more of your vulnerabilities and insecurities.

One day, while sitting at home in deep thought, I received a message from his ex-girlfriend stating that she needed to speak to me. I called her and she explained that he had been reaching out again, and he wants to meet up with her. All the while, he had been trying to rekindle our relationship. She had finally gotten over him and wanted me to meet up with him instead to teach him a lesson. So, she arranged the whole meeting and I proceeded to go to the bar in her place. When I arrived, he was sitting there waiting for her in his car. The look on his face was priceless when he saw me drive up. He sped off in his vehicle and kept calling me to explain what was going on. I wouldn't answer the phone, so he got mad. We ended up on a high-speed chase all over Houston.

I know that sounds crazy as hell, but yep, that was my life. He said that he was trying to fix our relationship and he needed to know what he did wrong in their relationship, so that he could do better for me. I am laughing at the BS as I type it. I was on such a roller coaster and I could not seem to get off. The whole situation was so exhausting, but I was addicted to figuring him out. I was trying to rationalize irrational behavior. Even the professionals have difficulty identifying the behaviors and end up in similar situations with Narcissists. I hoped I was wrong about the Narcissism and that maybe he was just Bi-polar or young and dumb. Something that he could take medication for and actually be cured. My self-esteem had reached an all-time low. I was so anxious and insecure, but life didn't stop for me to get it together, go figure.

It was finally that time! My baby girl arrived on November 8th. I was beyond happy. He was there during the birth, cut the cord and everything. My family and friends were in the room. It was such a joyous occasion. We took her home, and although it was hard having another child in the house, I was in love. The day I got home from delivering my baby, he let me know that he was traveling to see his brother. I was so confused. You mean to tell me I just had a baby, and you are leaving to go party with your brother?!?! REALLY?!?! He knew about my Post-partum depression, and how bad it got if I didn't have enough rest. I just said to myself, okay, that's what's up! As usual, I went into auto-pilot and took care of what I needed to. He left and went to Las Vegas, and I took care of my beautiful baby girl. When he got back he brought the usual gifts, to gloss over everything. He even asked me to move back in together, so he could help with the baby. Against my better judgement, I agreed.

We started searching for a place and ended up finding a really nice three bedroom. Of course, he was ecstatic, because we are "starting over." He was also close to graduating from college. I was so proud of him and his accomplishments. He was so smart and driven. During this time, he even got a promotion at his job, so we had more money coming in. He went and bought me a used SUV, because it was hard to fit all the children in my Nissan Altima. We started taking more and more trips. It was a happy time for us, but it didn't last long. I went out with some friends one night and received a call from my son, telling me I need to come home. He said that he saw my "prince charming," on my computer and he was going back and forth between my computer and his computer. I left the engagement and went home. I ended up finding out that he had put spyware on my computer to track my passwords, emails, etc. I had the receipt for the purchase as well in my possession. I asked him about it and he lied time after time. Even with the receipt in front of him.

I had even found an email where he was looking for daycare near his sister's house to take my children to Georgia without my knowledge. I could not believe it! It was like God was always showing me the secrets and lies, but I would still end up finding a way to move forward with him. Don't get me wrong, I was in love with this man. Even with all the stuff he put me through, I always thought that deep down inside he would eventually find God and we would ride off into the sunset together. You just visualized that huh?? Yeah me too. SMH...I started to believe that everything was happening because I was living with a man without being married. I said to myself maybe if we get married, he will be different. Maybe God will bless what we have, and I will be forgiven for my past and present. We started to talk more about marriage and our future together.

I should have known if it was too peaceful, soon chaos would follow. With a Narcissist, there is no such thing as peace. They love chaos and will create it whenever things get too quiet or they get bored. They get bored very easily. You find yourself walking on eggshells and unable to function normally, because you cannot predict their moods. You are just trying to do anything to keep them happy. One minute everything will be so good, and they are in love and the next minute, you are not good enough and they can have way better.

He started disappearing and going to strip clubs more, taking trips and not inviting me. He would plan the trip with his sister and her husband and just want to up and leave. When I would ask him about it, he would tell me, "oh you have the kids." I remember one disagreement we had, I was telling him that we were not going to continue being together the way that our relationship is going. As I was talking, all of a sudden, he rushed towards me and started choking me. I was standing in the bathroom with my two younger children. After he let go of my neck, he started to scream in my face with spit flying everywhere. He was in a complete rage. Then, out of the blue he started to bite me all over my face and neck, while foaming at the mouth. Our girls were screaming to the top of their lungs for him to stop. It was like he had totally blacked out. I'm pushing him away, and he is steadily coming at me, very aggressively. I don't know how, but eventually he calmed down, and left the house for the rest of the day.

I sat there just crying and trying to comfort my babies. I felt so confused. When they were finally calm and ready for bed, I took them to their room. I remember just going to my room, in my closet and just praying. I begged for God to guide me through this situation, because I was truly lost. I asked repeatedly, what had I done to deserve this. Knowing what I know now, this had nothing to do with God and everything to do with me and my insecurities, my need for perfection and validation, my lack of self-love. It took me a long time to figure these things out, but sometimes you meet people who are meant to show you yourself. The lessons suck and it's very painful, but with the help of God, the benefits are life changing. He will turn something that was meant to destroy you into your testimony. I learned that when the student is ready, the teacher will arrive, in God's perfect timing.

Chapter 10

There are several types of Narcissists. Not every Narcissist will get physical with their victims. I think this is where a lot of women get confused. Many Narcissist are satisfied with destroying you little by little with verbal and emotional abuse and constant manipulation. They are very subtle with their manipulation and games, until you totally lose touch with your reality. Some Narcissist harbor so much anger and self-hatred inside, that when they can no longer hide it, they totally unleash. When I would talk to him about what he did, he would make comments like "You made me so mad," or "I never laid a hand on you." He said it with so much conviction that I think he had really blocked everything out. It was so weird to me. If he wasn't getting physical, he was making belittling comments and telling me how other girls and exes would be better for him. He would take girls from television and tell me how me how much he likes the bigger booty girls or girls who were much younger than me. My self-esteem was totally taking a hit, but yet and still I stayed on the roller coaster.

School was such a struggle, but I was doing well. He was tutoring me in math, since that was never really my subject. He would sit down with me every day and help me with my homework. During those moments, I went through constant bouts of cognitive dissonance. I knew who he was behind the mask, but I thought in moments like this that maybe if I didn't make him so angry, he would not lash out. If I would just stop tripping over situations, maybe he won't feel the need to dominate and control me. I mean, he was coming home and spending time with me. We were always going on dates and doing things together. He was always texting and calling, unless he felt the need to play mind games, to make me feel confused and off balance.

It was funny though because he didn't jump on me all the time. I never knew when he was going to do it. We could be talking very calmly having a disagreement, and out of the blue he would be on top of me. He never did it in front of my boys though, but my oldest son knew what was happening. I still work on forgiving myself for letting my children go through what they did, because I know that it changed something within them. I was working so hard to make sure my children were taken care of by sacrificing myself for superficial things, and they would have been much happier living in a box, as long as their mother was safe. Also, the fact that I had been married before, I did not want the stigma of another failed marriage. If I would have known what I know now about people judging you regardless, I would have left a long time ago.

My "prince charming" decided that he would once again be taking a trip without letting me know or extending an invitation to me, so I sent him on his merry way along with his items to move elsewhere when he got back. Once again, he was going with his sister and her boyfriend, but I was not included. I was so tired of the bull crap and constant games. After he left, I started looking at our phone bill etc. While he is texting, me saying he loves me and wants to come back home, I'm seeing this random number popping up on my Verizon bill. I finally called the number and found out it was a young female that his brother hooked him up with from Las Vegas. She told me all the lies he was telling her about me. I'm lazy, he is paying my bills, he is only with me for the children, I'm crazy and unstable. The list goes on. Then she tells me that he is moving there to be with her. She was so happy and proud. At this point, I was like okay, let me call him. I contacted "prince charming," and he got back home so fast, that I forgot he was out of town. My petty behind called her with him in the background just to let her know, GIRL BYE! Jokes on me though, I should have let her have him...HA!

We talked that night after he got back from out of town, and of course he never admitted the truth and continued lying about the situation. He ended up moving to another apartment across town when I didn't agree to let him move back again. We stayed apart for a long period of time. He was angry that I did not believe his story about the girl from Las Vegas. He started to use the silent treatment again, trying to regain control over my feelings and emotions. It didn't affect me like it used to, so we ended up only communicating if it concerned our children. It was very peaceful at home. I was happy, and my children were all happy. School was going great and I was making so much progress in my life.

Of course, a Narcissist will not let you go that easily, especially if you are happy without them. If they see you moving on, they will start to **Hoover**, which they do flawlessly. Hoovering is a technique used by Narcissist to suck their victims back into a relationship with them. So basically, they can treat you bad, and abuse you, and once you leave or they discard you, they use this tactic to suck you right back in like a Hoover vacuum cleaner. You may get a playful text message out of the blue that says, "what's up boo?", "WYD?", or they claim to have sent a message to you by accident. They may even try to send a message about a shared experience, for example, "What was the name of the soul food restaurant we used to go to?"

The Narcissist will also use special occasions or catastrophic events to reel you back in. The message may read: "I just found out my aunt has cancer," or "I am not doing well and feel like I can't go on," or "I wish I could celebrate your birthday with you," or "remember our first Valentine's day together, and how happy we were?" You also may get the accidental call, where the phone dialed you without their knowledge. They will even call you to say, "did you just call me?" or "did I see you at the gym earlier?" The games are endless with them. I recall a message that I received, and it read: "Stop stalking me." I'm like wait, what?!?!?! It is there sick and twisted attempt to get a response and reaction from you.

EVERY Narcissist will Hoover at some point. The crazy thing is that it can be after a couple of days, weeks, months or even years. Some survivors have even been Hoovered a whopping 15 to 30 YEARS later! They never get tired! Don't get it twisted though, it has nothing to do with you, it is all about them and their selfish needs. Unfortunately, I learned all of this way after the fact.

With no communication, "prince charming" started to reach again. One day, he called and asked me on a date. I accepted the offer and we went to a very nice restaurant. When we arrived, he proceeds to talk to me about how he is so happy single. How he is doing so much better without me. At this point he had graduated from college, so he was feeling himself. His exact words were: "Look at me, I am now a bachelor with a Bachelor's Degree." It was a very laughable moment and our server could not contain his laughter. His humor was always very weird. I could not believe that he had invited me out to an expensive dinner, that he was paying for, to talk about how happy he is without me. I mean, who does that?! Anybody that knows me, understands, I was not passing up a good meal though. I just let him talk until he got tired and then I went home. Of course, after that dinner, we started hanging out again at each other's places. We got nice and comfortable back in the same old routine.

The honeymoon and love bombing started all over again. He ended up proposing to me, if that's what you call it. We were going to move into a brand-new house, but I knew I wasn't moving unless we got married. So, he gave me this half ass proposal like "are we going to get married or what?" and put the ring on my finger. We ended up getting married shortly thereafter. The day of our wedding was actually one of the happiest days of my life. He seemed like he was really going to take his role seriously. My "prince charming" even wrote "Just Married" on the back of our car, so that everyone would know. I just knew by us taking this huge step, something would change in our relationship. Oh, it did alright, but not exactly what I had in mind. I thought that he would finally see that I had his back, and he would learn to have mine. I hoped that God would bless our union, because we were no longer living in sin.

I really prayed that this step in our lives would change the past. We were on cloud nine on our wedding day. When I look back at our pictures, you would never know, based on our smiles, that we were in such a destructive and volatile relationship. It taught me that people can take pretty pictures, but that does not tell the story of what's behind closed doors. All that glitters is not gold. I remember waking up the next day and he did not even wear his wedding ring to work because he "forgot" (smile)...that should have been my first clue for what was up ahead, but I have always been maybe a little too optimistic for my own good.

Chapter 11

We ended up moving into our new home not far from our old apartment. New beginnings. Everything was going great. My children were growing, and they loved their new surroundings. Also, I finally graduated from college. I was so proud of myself because I graduated at the top of my class! With everything that I had been through, I was still able to reach my goal. I was so happy, but this caused a lot of issues because he thought I was trying to show him up. His exact words on my graduation day: "why do you have to be such an overachiever?" He would never make comments like this in front of anybody else, it was always when we were alone. Everybody thought he was the most supportive and loving husband.

After my graduation was over everything seemed to calm down a little bit. I was still riding on my high after obtaining my degree.

He was busy working on various projects at his job, so we had a lot of distractions, which was good. I should have known it was too quiet because all the manipulation started again. He loved to point out our age difference and how he could always get a younger woman. He talked about him wanting me to wear clothes that showed more skin like his ex-girlfriend used to. I was trying to keep up. I was turning every trick in the bedroom, but nothing was ever enough. I mean we had sex sometimes three times a day, and he would still accuse me of being with somebody else. We were even going to strip clubs, buying sex toys, and watching porn movies, and this still wasn't enough. I just could not seem to keep him happy.

I ended up enrolling at the University of Houston, so that I could obtain my Bachelor's degree. I knew that if I completed my program, we would have even more money coming into the household. I should have known this was going to create more conflict. We would argue often, because I paid too much attention to my children or my school work. He was content with us sitting in the room every evening, just me and him with the door closed. I constantly had to explain that the children had to eat, and they had homework etc. It was hard to keep in contact with my family and friends because he wanted ALL my time and attention. For example, If he saw me on the phone at any time, he would stare at me until I got off.

I ended up meeting a girl from work, and we started getting closer. She really helped me when it came to getting out of the house and having fun. He didn't like her though, so it started arguments whenever she came around. He absolutely hated anybody who took my attention away from him and he knew exactly how to get it back. Since he felt like my attention was elsewhere, the disappearing acts started again. He would say he was going one place, but the receipts said another. He was meeting females from his past secretly. There was one female who travelled all the way from Georgia to meet him, and I did not know about it until I found a text message and picture they took at a restaurant. Of course, he even lied about that, even with the picture in front of him. The cycle had started all the way over, and I couldn't handle it with everything I had on my plate.

My eyes had even started to wander, because I started wondering what it would be like to have a man who would treat me like a wife and partner. I was in a marriage, but I felt more alone than ever. During this time, his job was going well, and he was excelling. He was becoming a social butterfly, which was never his personality. I was usually the extrovert, but during this time, I was beginning to isolate myself from everybody. I just wanted to hide.

I was happy for him, but I didn't understand why he was only happy when I was depressed and depressed when I was happy. I didn't understand this until I read about the transference of energy between the Narcissist and the **Empath**. The Narcissist is often referred to as an energy vampire, because they project their sickness onto their victim. All their insecurities, feelings of worthlessness and depression has been transferred onto you, their empathetic victim. Making you appear to be the sick one. They are doing this day in and day out. Making you feel extremely tired and your anxiety will be at an all-time high, because you are trying to adjust to the hot and cold behavior of your partner.

You are more than likely experiencing **adrenal fatigue**. This usually happens, because your body cannot handle the constant state of fight and flight mode that most victims experience while trying to stay prepared for the next angry outburst or silent treatment they have grown accustomed to. This alone makes the Narcissist feel powerful and on top of the world. They have succeeded in making their abnormal behavior a normal part of your life. After years of abuse your health will start to deteriorate. I started having severe pain in my joints and was diagnosed with fibromyalgia, which I no longer have any symptoms of since leaving my abusive relationship. This type of rheumatic condition is very common for people who have experienced Narcissistic abuse. I was unable to get out of the bed sometimes, because it felt like I was hit by a Mac truck. If I took the medication for pain, I couldn't function at all and that caused more arguments within my relationship, because I was not giving him the proper amount of attention. He would tell me that he could find somebody else who would give him what he needed.

My memory was fading, and I couldn't remember or concentrate on what I was doing from day to day. It was hard to work and continue school, but I did the best I could to stay afloat. I often went into auto-pilot mode to fulfill my everyday responsibilities. I felt total despair most days, but I kept a smile on my face for the public because I was so ashamed of my situation behind closed doors.

I started getting up at 3:30 am every day to do school work and prepare for the day since I was taking mostly online classes. I was also caring for my four children. This gave me a new focus. It caused problems with my husband, but I promised myself that I was going to graduate. Not just graduate, but at the top of my class. I had to do this for not only myself but my children. During this time to add to my journey of pain, I also lost my father. This was a very trying time because although I just wanted to collapse, I could not because my father's affairs had to be handled. I ended up being gone for about 3 weeks from the time that I got the call regarding my father being in hospice, arranging his funeral and emptying out the house that I grew up in. I watched the first man in my life take his last breath. I held him, looked in his eyes in that moment and told him that we will be fine, and that he could go.

My father closed his eyes for the last time, and my heart broke into pieces. This was one of the most traumatic moments in my entire life. I had never felt heartbreak like that before. By the grace of God, I had my older sister by my side. During this time, I was still handling my school responsibilities, even from the hospital. My sister would take care of cleaning out my father's house while I was gone to take care of homework assignments and tests. Without being able to grieve, I had to return home where I had no support from my husband.

My husband took care of the kids while I was gone, which was a blessing. I was so happy to get back home and see my family. I knew that it was not easy for him to take care of them all by himself, so I appreciated him taking on the responsibility. When I got home, it was obvious that my husband was angry because I was gone for so long. He started to display passive aggressive behaviors to punish me. He would not comfort me at all during this time and told me to get over it because my father is gone. He told me that I didn't get along with my father anyway, so I should be fine. I remember lying in the bed just crying all night, my heart throbbing in my chest, and he laid beside me with his eyes open looking up at the ceiling and would not touch me or comfort me at all. I was devastated. The feelings that I had during that time are indescribable. I kept praying for strength to keep going and I did. I went back to my regular routine of work, school, and taking care of my babies. During this time of grief and hardship, a dream was born.

Chapter 12

The vision for Keeping It Light, my new business venture, changed my life and gave me a new focus and purpose. I ended up opening Keeping It Light, in memory of my father and this started my process of healing and moving forward. The business name, website and everything came to me in dreams. I started waking up even earlier, doing school work and creating my business. I had always wanted to be a business owner but never thought I would have the opportunity. As I began the process of healing and moving closer to my dreams, my relationship got worse.

One day I woke up and I no longer recognized the woman who was looking back at me. I had dark circles under my eyes. I had also lost weight. I started trying to fix myself, because he told me I was the problem. He appeared to be fine, so it had to be me. I would go to counseling session after counseling session, but I would often not tell them how deep the abuse went, so they could only give me advice based on how transparent I was. I kept a lot hidden trying to protect the reputation of my abuser and the picture of a perfect relationship that I painted in my mind. The one thing that all the counselors agreed on was the problem was not from me. I tried to get him to go with me. He said that he would go, if it would help me get fixed. We even went a couple of times together, but once the counselor identified his issues, he would stop going.

During this time, I started to meditate, and this became my life line. In between reading self-help books, listening to Oprah, Les Brown, and Lisa Nichols, I started to get stronger. I would join meditation groups, and empowerment groups. Anything that allowed me to forget about my current circumstances, but you know I paid dearly for this time away from him. We even argued about me meditating and praying too much. I would beg for him to join me, but that never happened.

My husband woke me up one day to let me know his brother was going through a divorce and needed to pass through for a couple of days. He was from Las Vegas but had lived in Houston previously. I had only met him a couple of times by then, even though my husband and I had been together for six years. When he arrived, everything was fine until I realized he was staying longer than my husband and I had discussed. I asked my husband about this and he let me know that he was staying as long as he needed too. I didn't have a problem with him staying, but my husband told me that he made the decision and that I had no say in the matter. My son had been displaced from his room and was sleeping on the hard floor, because we were told it was only for a couple of days.

This started so much friction, and I felt bad because his brother was really respectful and helped around the house. We would talk about various topics during the day, and he would give me business tips since he was a successful business owner prior to his divorce. He gushed about how he thought my business was going to take off and it was going to be a success. He had looked at my website when I had accidentally left it up on a different computer at my mother in law's house. He complimented me about my business and the direction I was going in. This made me feel good, and helped me progress further towards my vision, but it caused more disconnect between me and my husband. He started to be angry with me for no reason. He began to be more passive aggressive with his behaviors. He always wanted to make sure nobody saw or recognized what he was doing. My oldest son was starting to get a clearer picture. My husband knew he was watching, so he was more careful about what he would do outside of the room.

During this same time, he invited is sister and her husband to stay with us as well without telling me. They had already made the plan and would be coming within the next couple of days. I knew this was going to cause more problems, because when he got with his sister, he liked to show off. He would talk down to me, and she thought she could do the same. I would read messages that they wrote back and forth dogging me to one another. She always thought I didn't know, but through my growth process, I realized some negativity did not deserve a response.

I welcomed them into my home, and it only took a day to go south. My husband and I ended up having a knock down drag out fight at the strip club. Yes, I said the strip club! It was all of them against me, but that day I wasn't backing down. Hell no! They were in my house disrespecting me and thinking that I was going to take it lying down. Oh, I just had a flashback of that day! We ended up going home separately, and once I got there the situation escalated. So I went upstairs to my room, and he tried to trap me in the bathroom, so nobody could hear what was happening. He started pushing me and getting very aggressive, but I was able to get out before it could get worse. I went downstairs where everybody was sitting and informed them that if he put his hands on me again, I would press charges and he would go to jail. I contacted my family to let them know the situation, and from there everything calmed down.

His sister and her husband only stayed a couple more days after that, but the situation only got worse. After they left I was doing my homework on the brand-new computer he purchased for me prior to his family coming. He always did nice things to make up for hitting me or treating me badly. I was sitting at the table doing homework, and he wanted to argue. I refused to argue that day and ignored him and kept typing. He walked over closer to me, slammed my computer closed and knocked it all the way across the floor. He responded to the pieces flying everywhere by saying, "now how will you do your business or homework?" These types of incidents were increasing, so I stayed on guard to make sure I was always ready for his angry outburst.

One day, while standing in the closet, we started arguing about me not showing him enough gratitude for everything he has ever done for me. He got very angry for my "ungratefulness" and trapped me inside of the closet. My kids were standing next to me, but that did not change his behavior. He began to hit and bite me. He bit me all over my face, while my daughters are screaming and begging him to stop. My oldest daughter was able to get my phone, and by the grace of God, my sister called at that exact moment. She was able to tell my sister what was going on, and that her father had hit me. When he realized that my sister was on the phone, he calmed down and left the house. When he got back he was quiet, but I just couldn't get over him putting his hands on me again.

I was officially tired. Nobody should have to live like this from day to day. I ended up packing my stuff while my husband was at work, and his brother was gone for the day. My children and I moved in with my mother for about two weeks, but she lived too far from their schools etc. He ended up apologizing and begging me to come back home. I think he only did that because I took the cable boxes, when I left (a little humor). Just Petty! When I got back home the peace would only end up lasting for 3 or 4 days. He ended up getting angry about something I said, and he tried to kick the door down again. It was one angry outburst after another. I ended up finally calling the police, when it got to out of hand. He would still act crazy even with the police there, but they would do everything in their power not to take him to jail, since he was a young and educated black male. Those were the officer's words exactly.

Chapter 13

We decided it was time for him to get his own place. I did not know that this was the plan all along, for him and his brother to get a place. They ended up getting a place not too far from our home. We did not talk, and I would only deal with him for visitation for the kids. He would play games even with the limited amount of contact. The children would be waiting for him, and he would call last minute and let me know he was not coming. He wouldn't give me money for the children, and once again it was sink or swim for me. I have always been a hustler, so you know what happened. Your girl held it down and kept it moving.

Shortly after he saw that I was okay without him, he and his brother ended up on bad terms, so he wanted to move back home with me, which he did, and I got back on the roller coaster once again. It was against my better judgement, but I did it anyway. He showed his a** on the first day he got there...Imagine that! Everything started all over again. When you take a Narcissist back time and time again you are making them feel more powerful. You are also proving to them that you are powerless. All they need from you is Narcissistic Supply. They don't love you, because they are not capable. Basically, they were able to fool you and get you to take them back, so the games are going to get worse. People who are Empaths can't understand that the Narcissist will never love you. It's all about power and control.

Shortly after he moved back in, my husband started traveling more and more to Atlanta. He was a HUGE Atlanta Falcons fan, so he would go with his family to the games. One day, I got an eerie feeling when he told me about another potential unplanned trip to Atlanta. During this time, we had started looking to purchase a house, because we wanted to own instead of rent. We were applying for loans and everything, that's how serious we were about the process. On this day, he had left his work computer at home by accident. It was like the computer was calling my name. NIIIIISSSSSAAAAAA! I opened it and went straight to work. I cracked the password to his email but was not ready for what I saw.

There was one particular email, which stopped me dead in my tracks. It was from a company in Atlanta, thanking him for completing his round of interviews. According to the email, he had just finished up his third interview, and they would be making a decision soon. Yes, I said THIRD. I was shocked! It took me a moment to catch my breath. I just sat there for a minute. All of this time we were looking for a house in Houston, he was planning to move to Atlanta. He had not even told me he had applied for the position, let alone interviewed multiple times and was at the end of the process. I was floored! When he got home we argued and he tried to lie, but I had the email in my hand. He explained that he didn't tell me because he didn't want to put any pressure on me without knowing whether or not he had the job..blah, blah, blah.

The feeling of betrayal was so strong. I ended up falling into a deep depression. I found out that all of his family and friends knew about the job and interviews, everybody but me. I just couldn't understand how he could do this and act like it was normal behavior. About a week after me finding the email, he ended up receiving a call from the company to make an official offer for the job. He acted like he was giving me the option to decide whether he was going to take it or not. I was so hurt. My family was in Houston. My son would have to stay in Houston, because he was one of the top wrestlers in the state of Texas. My son wanted to get a scholarship, so that he could wrestle in college. His father also lived in Houston and did not want our son leaving the state. Don't get me wrong, this was a great opportunity for my husband's career and would ultimately set him up for further success. I just couldn't shake the fact that he had applied, interviewed and planned to take a position all behind my back. I felt physically sick. I couldn't believe that within the whole process he didn't even consider me and that I had just opened my business. I had worked so hard on getting it set-up and off the ground. He knew I was trying to finish up my Bachelor's degree. He didn't even think about my children, our children and the position it would put everybody in.

I cracked under the pressure and ended up in the hospital for a while. To be completely honest, I tried to commit suicide. It wasn't just the current situation, but a combination of several years of abuse, manipulation, betrayal, and deceit. My self-esteem had taken a real hit and I started to really think I could not go on. Anybody who has been in a relationship with a Narcissist, can maybe relate to this feeling. They break down all of your defenses. They chip away at your self-esteem bit by bit. You start to cater to their needs, because their behavior is teaching you that your needs don't matter. You stop living and just start existing. You realize that as long as you continue to admire, praise and show them attention, everything will be beautiful, but the minute you step out of character, you will pay dearly.

You are also being blamed for the whole breakdown of the relationship. Narcissists use a manipulation tactic called **projection**, which shifts the blame for every negative event in your relationship from them onto you. If you start pointing out their behavior, they will flip it and accuse you of the same behavior. For example, if you call them a liar, they will accuse you of lying. Also, if you accuse them of being abusive, they will flip it and accuse you of being abusive. You don't realize until it's too late that you have been annihilated by your abuser.

When dealing with a Narcissist, your body stays in a heightened state of awareness, which keeps you constantly exhausted and off balance. You no longer know what food, clothes or movies you like. They have told you what is acceptable and unacceptable in their world of perfection. The extrovert becomes the introvert. Nothing you do is ever good enough for them and you will always miss the mark. They will make sure you know that they are the center of your universe and will punish you if you ever forget. It's like you are running an eternal marathon trying to keep them happy, and they keep moving the finish line. You will never win their imaginary race!

All I wanted was a two-parent household for my children and a sense of normalcy. Even with everything that had happened, I still couldn't give up. Unfortunately, that's my personality to fight until I have no more fight in me. I didn't realize that this fight would almost take me out of this world. Fortunately, I was able to meet some beautiful women during my hospital visit. We shared our stories and leaned on each other for strength. We prayed together. They opened my eyes to the subject of spiritual warfare, and I realized that what I was fighting was deeper than what I could see. That's the reason I felt trapped in a cycle that would not end. I had always been a fighter, but in this situation, I felt defeated. Even though I felt defeated, something inside of me wouldn't let me fully give up. I got out of the hospital, and quickly got back to my life. I had children to take care of, and grades to maintain. I wanted to graduate at the top of my class again, and I was not going to let the devil stop me no matter what.

Chapter 14

I ultimately made the decision to move to Atlanta, Georgia with my husband. Even though I knew his family, would be a problem and I was going to unfamiliar territory. My son made the decision to stay in Houston, which was so hard for me. I talked to my husband and decided that he would go ahead of me for 8 months, so that my son could finish the school year and I could complete my degree without any interruptions. He would come pretty much every other weekend to spend time with us and we would go to Atlanta as well. We would talk on the phone, but there was an obvious disconnect between us. I just could not understand the hot and cold treatment. One day he was in love with me and the next day, it was as if everything I did annoyed him.

Out of the blue, he decided that we would purchase a house before I arrived. I was apprehensive, because I thought it was rushed, but he had already made up his mind. He found a beautiful home (five bedrooms/3 bathrooms), that had just been built inside of a brand-new subdivision. The process moved pretty quickly, and we became homeowners. I guess, I should say he became a home owner, because my name was supposed to be added to the deed, but it never happened. Funny thing is I never pushed it because in the back of my mind, I already knew the end of our story. I just needed time for my heart and mind to catch up with the feeling I had in my gut.

The time finally arrived for us to move. My kids were excited about the move and he had found one of the best school districts for them to be in. I finished school and graduated at the top of my class. I was so happy and felt like, maybe we could get back on track being in a new environment with no distractions. I told you I was a little too optimistic for my own good sometimes (smile). I started looking for a job within my field. It took a while, and this caused major friction between us. He was telling me to take my time to find a job, and not to settle but I found out he was telling everybody else a totally different story. His family members started making rude comments to me about finding a job and posting job ads on their Facebook pages for me to see. I was also told by another family member that his family was telling everybody that I was using him for his money. The same man that I took care of while he was unemployed; imagine that.

He realized that maybe we should have waited to purchase the house until after I found a job. We started arguing a lot more. I started putting pressure on myself, so I took the next thing that came my way. Horrible mistake. I ended up working in the male/female prison system. For those who know me, they know this was definitely not the move for me, especially in Atlanta. I ended up leaving there and we decided I would open my business again in Georgia.

I hustled until I had everything in place. I was in the process of creating a professional commercial and had so much support from family and friends. I started securing clients and making money right away, which is pretty good for just getting started, especially in an unfamiliar market. I started networking and meeting people. I made new friends. I was in my own element, since I am a natural born entrepreneur. I was enjoying my new-found success, but I should have known my happiness would not last for long with a Narcissist around.

My husband started talking down to me and treating me badly. He began withholding money and it made it hard to keep my business running. He started making belittling remarks towards me even in front of others. He kept saying I didn't love him like I used too. I knew exactly what he meant. I was finding my way again, and he did not like that. He was also surprised that I already had friends from my past that lived in Atlanta, so we all reconnected. He would leave me while he would go hang out with his family, without inviting me. If I was invited his family felt like that was the time to get things off their chest, that of course he had told them about me. I knew that once the mask falls off in front of others and they no longer are hiding, it's only going to get worse. I started to mentally prepare myself to leave, so I found a local counselor to help me with moving forward.

My new counselor carefully listened to my story, he looked at me for a moment. I could see he was trying to carefully frame what he was about to tell me. After a few seconds of awkward silence, he told me point blank that I was with a Narcissist and if I did not leave, this man was going to destroy every part of me. He read out loud all my positive qualities and accomplishments that he wrote down during our sessions. He explained to me that medication was not what I needed and if I would make the move to end my relationship, my outlook on my life would change and my depression would lift. He taught me communication tactics that would empower me when dealing with my husband until I decided to leave. Something clicked in me on that day. I started to see myself through my counselor's lens and it helped me to look in the mirror and remember who I was before I met my husband. I knew he was right.

I started making plans soon after and praying for strength. I decided to start an empowerment group for female entrepreneurs, which grew beyond my expectations.. This set my husband off because once again, I was getting my happiness outside of him. He didn't consider the fact that he was going out with his family and a lot of times I was being left out. I started doing video interviews with inspirational women for my new series, "Inspirational Women of 2016". I was enjoying myself and starting to feel like my old self again. I had no idea that while I was working on preparing us as a group for our journey towards success, I was gaining the strength and confidence that I needed to finally end my relationship. I knew that the end was near because our relationship became even more volatile.

Chapter 15

On the day of my birthday I was so excited to find out what he had planned for me. I just knew that he had at least put all the drama aside for my special day. HA! I quickly found out that he had a plan alright, but it wasn't the picture that I had painted in my mind. He decided that we were not going anywhere for my birthday and he wanted to rehash past drama. He had heard me getting phone calls about what the plans were so people could meet us and his mood changed. We began to argue, and something clicked inside of me. I got quiet. In that moment I decided I was not going to get on the emotional roller coaster for the usual ride that we go on.

Something inside of me had changed because I got up, put my clothes on and decided to go out whether he was going or not. He quickly got dressed and we went to meet my friends. Once we got around them it was all love. He acted like he was the most loving husband ever, but they knew better. It is very common for Narcissists to ruin birthdays and holidays, especially if you are the center of attention on that particular day. Also, if they know you are looking forward to a specific holiday, pay attention as the day gets closer. The chaos will begin, just in time to ruin the big day. They hate to see others genuinely happy, because they have a void within themselves that keeps them from feeling normal human emotions. They also have to find a way to make everything about them.

Another incident that transpired and was pretty much the end for me. He surprised me with an unplanned trip to his mother's house. Yes, I said his mother's house (smile). Of course, he had already made the plan without speaking to me or considering my schedule. I was so busy with everything I was working on, so I did not want to go. He would not take no for an answer. Plus, I did not like his mother, and he knew this. I had respectfully dealt with this woman who was constantly belittling and talking about me to any and everybody who would listen to her for almost nine years. I would inform my husband about what was being said, but he would say there was nothing he could do about it.

On this day after we arrived, she finally felt comfortable enough to say what she had felt about me for years. It was almost as if they had planned the visit just for that reason. I realized that all the negative things being said had come from the man who I called my "husband." I was shocked at the things he had shared with her. He had even told her I gave him an STI. I got so angry in that moment and ended up acting a fool. I regret that I gave her what she wanted, by responding to her negativity, but it felt good to finally defend myself.

He allowed his mom that day to disrespect me, and he asked me the question "what do you want me to do about it?" I looked at him directly in his eyes, and said, "Don't do a damn thing, because I'm done with your weak ass anyway." In that moment, I lost any respect for him that I had left. I was hurt, but it is what it is, and this was not the time to display the feelings of betrayal that I felt. I tried to leave, but they hid my keys and would not give them to me.

My children who heard all the commotion, contacted my son in Houston. My son ended up contacting the police all the way from

Houston. The police arrived, and they tried to act like I was the culprit. The officer after speaking to them, realized what was happening, and told me to leave my husband and go back home on my own turf, which was three hours from where I was. He told me to take the car and let him figure out his own way home. I heard the officer loud and clear, what he said and what he didn't say, so I left and went home. How my husband knew I was home, I will never know, but he arrived home a couple of hours after I did. I found out after the fact, that he had taken his father's car, and left shortly after he realized I had left back to Atlanta.

That night he came home very angry, and physically attacked me. He jumped on top of me choking me and threatened to end my life. He had his knee in my chest, while choking me. He looked in my eyes and told me "I am going to kill you one day." He said: "you think I am playing, but you are going to die." Although he had threatened me many times before, the look in his eyes signaled to me that this time was different. His eyes had turned so dark, that I barely recognized him. He eventually calmed down and fell asleep. I laid there awake all night thinking of my next move. I decided before the sun came up that I was leaving my marriage.

The next morning, I snuck out with my children and went to the court house to get a restraining order. I also ended up moving in with a friend temporarily. It really put a strain on me because I ended up an hour away from where I operated my business. I was no longer close to the children's school or daycare, so when a client would call last minute it made it hard to get there on time. This whole situation was so hard for me to swallow. I stayed with my friend for a while and then I moved into an extended stay. He kept trying to get back with me during this time, sending me emails and messages through friends, but I was done.

I didn't end up going further with the restraining order because I didn't want him to lose his job or not be able to see his children. I was gone for about three weeks before, he informed me that if I returned home, he would leave and go stay with his sister. I packed the children up and went home thinking he would keep his word and leave when we got there. The minute I got back home, and put my bags down, he informed me that he wasn't leaving, and the accusations of infidelity started. We went on like this for about a week and I decided to call it quits once and for all. I just couldn't take it anymore. It had almost been nine years and it was only getting worse.

Chapter 16

I went to sleep that night but woke up with a feeling I couldn't quite describe. I knew it was the day. All the days prior, I felt weak, sad, my self-esteem had hit an all-time low, but today I felt strong. I was a woman with a purpose. A woman on a mission. I had no idea what was coming next, but I knew that day I was going to be moving on from my destructive marriage to a Narcissist. My marriage had almost destroyed me. I went from a beautiful, confident woman who was always sure of herself to an insecure, depressed, anxious woman who thought she should just be dead.

When I remembered who I used to be, the game changed. I thought that woman would never ever be back, but I looked in the mirror and, on that day, Nisaa Abdul-Rahman reappeared. I realized that I had given up until this particular day. God said to me, **"It's time to make your move, you are ready."** I took a deep breath and did just that. It was game time!

I called him to meet me at Starbucks after work because I did not want to be in a place for him to hit me. After he arrived, and we talked briefly, I let him know that I was done with the marriage. Of course, he cried and professed his love for me. Told me he knew I was going big places, and that he didn't want to be left behind.

He said that he was afraid I would fly and be successful without him. I found this ironic since he told me for years, that I was lazy and unmotivated. Your girl finally stepped out on faith that day. God, held me in the palm of his hands. I jumped off the imaginary cliff of my marriage and although it felt like my fall was endless, I never touched the ground, by the grace of God. He left me without any monetary support, but I was able to get a lawyer right away. In situations where you have no choice, you become creative. I called each of my family and friends and asked them to send me a donation to help me pay for my lawyer. Everybody who knew about the abuse that I experienced, sent me money and I was able to secure a lawyer.

I quickly filed for divorce. My lawyer turned out to be one of the biggest blessings that God gave me during this journey. She was one of my biggest supporters, she believed in me and my strength to overcome the obstacle that seemed hopeless at the time. She would talk to me even after her office hours and give me support during my darkest times. Despite my fear of the unknown, I moved full speed ahead. I made the tough decision to close my business, since I had to move from the area that I started the business in, and I would have to virtually start all over rebuilding my clientele in the new area. Remember, I am still pretty new to Georgia, so this made everything a little more complicated since

I was in an unfamiliar territory. Also, I was not receiving consistent financial support from my husband. My abuser still tried to control and manipulate me throughout the divorce process, but once I become determined to do something, there is no stopping me. He would say things like "you need me", "you can't make it without me," or "you will never find a house like the one I bought you" and "our marriage can work if you learn to love me more."

He would purposely miss payments on the house and I would receive threatening letters about them foreclosing on the house that me and my children were living in. He even tried to get me to forego anything through the courts, so that we can agree on our own terms. Fortunately, I had already studied the manipulation tactics used by a Narcissist during the divorce process, and this was one of the first tactics they warned of. He even tried to tell me he would only pay me $800 a month and he was not going to pay anything further for our two children. By this time, I was done playing games with him, and it was time to handle business, straight up. I was no longer going to allow him to control and manipulate the situation.

Even during this time, he would come over to get the kids and search through my panty and bra drawers to see what was missing. He would respond that he knew I was having sex with other people because certain pieces were not there, so they had been used. He would also come over unannounced using his key to gain access to the house at odd hours of the night.

One of my closest friends had my locks changed because she was so worried about his behavior and actions towards me. I started meeting him in the garage with the children's bags instead of him coming into my home. This changed the game and gave me back some of the control over my life. I started setting boundaries that he could not cross. I was going to get my life back, by any means necessary. The stress that I endured during this time was unbearable, but I knew I would be homeless before ever going back to the torture that I was freed from.

I stopped getting shocked by his behavior and started preparing for it, so that I could protect me and my children. This man even told his lawyer to give me and the kids one month to get out of our marital home, knowing we had nowhere to go or the financial means. What he failed to realize is I serve a mighty God. He blessed me in less than a month with a brand new four bedroom/three-bathroom house and all the finances to make that move. So, I ended up with the house my husband said I would never have again. Look at God!

I was working again, so life was looking brighter. I fell in love with teaching children. It was so therapeutic during my healing process. There is nothing like receiving hugs of appreciation from children, for doing something that is natural for you. Children telling you how much they love you. From Kindergarten to Twelfth grade, the children helped me to move forward every day. I learned so many powerful lessons about myself during this time. I opened myself up for God to start working on me. I was finally ready for the hard part, self-evaluation. I worked on not only forgiving my husband for what happened, but also taking responsibility for my part in the relationship. I had to admit and ask forgiveness for saying and doing things that I was not proud of during and after our relationship. I had to also work on forgiving myself for staying in such a toxic situation for so long.

I realized that I didn't love myself and felt unworthy. It was so hard, and sometimes I just wanted to give up, but I kept praying and moving forward. Sometimes all I could do was lay on the floor and cry. It really was a second at a time for me. I learned to be patient with myself and to treat myself the same way I would treat a friend in the same position.

Activities that I lost my passion for during my marriage, I started doing again. For example, my ex would always complain about my cooking during our marriage, so I became self-conscious and stopped enjoying the creative aspect of cooking. In order to break free from that mindset, I started trying new recipes and my children absolutely loved the meals that I would make. I started wearing my hair in styles that made me feel good. I put more color in my wardrobe. I even got rid of all the furniture we purchased together, so that I could go pick out what I wanted without being told how bad my taste is. Guess what?!?!? I even picked out my own brand of groceries. Imagine that! I know it sounds funny, but these are examples of how your whole personality is erased in a Narcissistic relationship. You become unrecognizable not only to yourself but to those who know you best.

My ex used to say I was not a good driver for long trips, so I took a road trip to Houston and guess what.... I drove the full 14 hours with only a few breaks. I also went hiking and climbed to the very top of a waterfall. The chains that once held me down, were slowly breaking. My children and I talked a lot more and I realized how happy they finally were with our transition. They told me they saw a lot more than I thought they did. So, while I thought I was doing them a favor by staying, I was only delaying the inevitable and causing more pain for everybody. A repeat of what I saw in my past. I had to have those difficult conversations with my older children. They explained that they were so proud of me and the woman that I am becoming, but we also had to address the past. That was very difficult to rehash, but it was necessary for the healing process.

Even though everything was coming together for me, I can honestly say I was not prepared for the roller coaster or as many refer to it as the healing process after Narcissistic Abuse, that I had to ultimately face. I could finally stop holding my breath, since I had a stable place to live for me and my children. They loved their new schools, daycare and neighborhood. Most of all they loved the drama free environment.

I went no contact with my ex and would only communicate by email if it was regarding our children. Setting the boundary of no contact and separating myself completely from him and his 'flying monkeys' saved my life. I no longer had to hear him belittling me and pointing out that he was 'paying my rent by paying me child support'. I no longer had to be questioned about who I was dating and whether I was having sex with other people. I prayed for God to remove our soul ties. The shift was not only obvious to me but everybody around me as well. I knew that I still had a long way to go, but life was really starting to look brighter for me and my children.

Those who have encountered any type of Narcissistic abuse can attest that sometimes the aftermath of the abuse is worse than the actual abuse. It's when the fog clears, and you realize the true evil that you encountered, the feeling of devastation truly hits you. It's like a roller coaster ride that you are stuck on. One day you are laughing, and the next day you are crying. You literally cycle between all the stages of grief over and over again. Sometimes the only thing you can do is lay in the bed and cry. I'm not talking just tears, I'm talking that ugly, from the pit of your stomach cry. Sometimes it takes everything in you to get up and just take a shower or take care of basic necessities. Your mind won't turn off. It's quiet, and you are thinking about everything that you endured. It's like a movie that won't stop playing.

You realize that your entire relationship was based on a lie and never existed, because a Narcissist is incapable of real love. Your self-esteem is at an all-time low, you feel worthless, and sometimes even suicidal. People don't really know what you went through because your physical scars have healed; if only they could see the bruises of the mind and soul destroyed by a Narcissist.

The Narcissist has more than likely left you facing financial ruin and this is done to make you suffer even more, because the basic human suffering after a break up is not enough, they lack empathy, so they keep driving the knife deeper and deeper. Not many people understand what Narcissism is and really don't want too because it's a deep dark place for the mind to visit. I know some of the sadistic mind games and manipulation that I encountered, if someone would have told me they went through it prior to me learning about Narcissism, I never would have believed them. It's truly beyond anything I ever would have imagined and I'm a Criminal Justice major. I have even counseled Doctors and Psychologist, who have been tricked into relationships with Narcissists.

We tend to throw around the term loosely and associate it with a conceited or vain person who takes a lot of selfies or is only concerned about themselves. Those are some traits of Narcissism, but it gets so much deeper. It's one of the greatest forms of evil. It's as if the Narcissists' of the world have their own play book and share notes. All the stories of victims match sometimes detail by detail. When you study about Narcissism, you often read about them using the same phrases, lies, and manipulation tactics to dismantle and destroy their victim piece by piece. I know Christians refer to it as the Jezebel spirit. I can definitely identify with that.

Breaking up with a Narcissist is far from a regular break up. This person has intentionally shattered your soul. If there is a such thing as hell on earth, the experience will be while dealing with a Narcissist and the aftermath. You have to claw yourself back to the top from the depths of hell. The sad thing about it is they are still abusing you even after they are no longer there. We already have talked about the smear campaign that they started years before you broke up, so nobody will believe your story anyway. They will go as far as even trying to turn your own family and friends against you. The Narcissist wants you to feel true isolation and despair. They have come to kill, steal and destroy and will not stop until you free yourself and give yourself over to the Most High. God is the only one that can bring you out. If it were not for God, I don't think I would be here and in my right mind.

You have to fight like you have never fought before and still maintain normalcy for both you and your children. Many say you are weak because you stayed. Yeah right! If you have endured a Narcissistic Abusive Relationship and made it out alive, that word can NEVER be associated with you. You have conquered probably one of the hardest things you will ever conquer in this world. You have to start over from scratch recreating yourself. I compare it to building the foundation of a house and laying each brick carefully in its proper place. It's an everyday second by second challenge. I wish I could say minute by minute or day by day, but if you have endured this soul shattering type of abuse, you know exactly what I mean.

It's hard to be around people. It's hard to work on your job. You are enduring one of the worst forms of **Post-Traumatic Stress Disorder.** You are second guessing yourself and replaying constantly every negative thing that the abuser said and did to you. You are just cycling day in and day out, until one day you realize that your experience can help others. We often ask "why me God?" and on this particular day I received my answer. God said, "why not you?" He put me through this fire because he knew not only would I come out like a true warrior, he knew I would use my experience to help other women come out of it as well. He knew that even while I was in pain, my love for helping others heal would help me to heal myself. He knew that being a natural educator, I would not only teach people about the disorder, but also how to not stay stuck in the cycle of self-loathing and despair that will never end.

I started making videos and opened a group for women. I started receiving emails and messages from women and men from all over the world who have encountered Narcissistic abuse or wanted to learn more about the disorder. The number of victims is astronomical. I had a new network of people I could talk to, who shared my experience. This changed the whole direction of my life. I knew that my life would never be the same, and God used my heartbreak to help me find my purpose.

When I finally left my abusive relationship one of the hardest things was processing the reality of what I had been through. I realized how many traumatic events I had blocked out to protect my sanity. I heard many different opinions from well meaning, but uninformed people about what I had been through and how I could start dating as a way to get over it. You have to be very careful of the information that you take into your spirit. People who have never encountered a Narcissist or have not educated themselves can only give you insight based on their own understanding or lack thereof.

You will hear statements like "the narcissist chose you because you are weak." This is the furthest thing from the truth, so please don't allow that to become a part of your reality. If you have studied who and what a Narcissist is they are very careful about choosing their target. They get bored very quickly, so the target has to keep their interest at some level. If you are too easy a target they will discard you right away without any explanation. They will just disappear and ghost you.

Some Narcissists require the best of the best to keep their fragile intact. This usually includes the flashiest cars, nicest houses, and most influential jobs. They always have to feel like they are on top of the world or doing better than others. That means he looks for a woman who he can show off, a trophy girl. She is smart, beautiful and ambitious but unsure of herself. He is impressed by something about her, and he will mirror exactly what it is, if you watch him very carefully.

Although she is dynamic in her own right, she is still looking for love and validation and he can smell it all over her. She is willing to dim her light to make her man shine brighter. She is willing to put her dreams on the back burner to allow him to fulfill his. He is fine with you as long as you don't do anything better than him that makes him feel inferior or inadequate. You can get attention, but never too much. Once you cross the line and he feels threatened, you have reached the point of no return. You have caused a **Narcissistic Injury** (a perceived threat to a narcissist's self-esteem or self-worth) and this will awaken the **Narcissists'**

Pathological Envy. The Narcissist feels entitled and always has to feel above everyone else. When this does not happen, or you do something that makes the Narcissist feel insignificant or less superior, this causes an injury to their fragile ego and you become a threat. What used to be one of your traits that the Narcissist idealized and bragged about to others, he will start to point them out to both you and others as your 'flaws' that he has to endure.

He will start to minimize your accomplishments to not only you, but everybody inside and outside of your circles. This includes friends, family, co-workers, and anybody else that will listen, because you have threatened his false sense of grandiosity and superiority. These scary combinations of rage and envy usually create a very dangerous situation for the victim. Since more than likely the victim has not told too many people about the abuse, this further isolates them and allows the abuser full control over the situation. The abuser who is usually well put together, charming, and sure of himself to the people on the outside, he will now let the mask completely fall off for those on the inside of the house. His anger and rage can play out in many different ways, but the ultimate goal of the Narcissist is to destroy you at all cost.

You have stepped outside of the box they built specifically for you and are beyond their control. You are gaining happiness outside of them, accomplishing your goals and daring to see a future. HUGE MISTAKE. You have now become a TRUE target, unbeknownst to you. I remember when I finally went back to school and graduated Summa Cum Laude with both of my degrees and opened my business, this was the first time that he did not even try to hide his hate and disdain for me. He told me that I was trying to show him up and outshine him, he gave me the silent treatment during some of those happiest times. In front of people he was so proud of me, but when we were alone it was a different story. He was very careful about others seeing him without his mask.

Usually in the house, I went through hell if he felt any type of slight whether intentional or unintentional. He would sometimes bite me all over my face and neck, kick me, punch me and tell me how if I would trust him and be a better wife he wouldn't get so angry. Sometimes he would even threaten to kill me. I would ask him to get help but he would say things like "I didn't do anything wrong" or "I never touched you," which is a classic statement made by Narcissists. We would go to the counselor because as he would say "I needed to be fixed, and he would help in any way that he can". He would wait until people came around, mind you he had already told them negative things about me, and he would start drama and sit back so innocently. When I would respond to what he had said or done, of course under the table, he would tell them see, "I told you she was unstable and crazy." He would tell them "do you see what I have to deal with?"

Their manipulation never ends. You always know that if it gets too quiet, chaos is soon to follow, the Narcissist hates the normal everyday mundane tasks of life, they cannot function, so the cycle of abuse starts all over again. After the cycle ends for the moment, the love bombing phase, expensive trips and gifts begin. They love you again and it feels amazing because they have beat you down so bad and you think just maybe this time is different.

We went through the vicious cycle of violence for almost nine years. I put him out and moved on so many times, but he would hoover and lie about how much he wants his family and I would end up right back in the abusive situation again. Only for him to start treating me bad on the same day he moved back in. I just could not understand what I was dealing with. I realized that I could identify so many things in other people's relationships but was blind to mine. Don't get me wrong, I knew something was off, but I had no idea that I had only hit the surface.

Although I knew my husband had issues, I thought if I just kept praying that God would fix my marriage. I thought if I worked on myself, we would get back on track. I wanted so badly for my children to live in a two-parent household, even if it meant that I had to sacrifice myself. I now understand how crippling that mindset is, but when you are in an abusive situation, your brain just goes into survival mode. You even find yourself protecting your abuser at all cost.

Chapter 17

As I think back on my relationship and how I ever attracted such a sick person in my life, memories from my past began to haunt me. I am not going to go into detail in this particular book, but my past included mental and emotional abuse. I was pre-wired to accept this type of behavior. Although everybody knows me as this strong, independent, don't take no crap type of chick, that vulnerable little girl who always wanted to be loved and protected is still very much a part of me. I never really processed my past abuse, so in a way, I think the relationship forced me to not only heal my present, but also heal my past. I learned that I attract a certain type of person based on the energy I am transmitting into the universe. I realized that if I didn't break the generational curse and deal with my issues, this may be a path that my daughters will be subjected to as well. That thought alone stopped me dead in my tracks.

I realized that not only was I attracting negative intimate relationships, but also friendships. This took me on a long journey of healing, cleansing and rediscovery of my purpose. I started reevaluating all my relationships. I stopped dating. I became celibate. I started setting personal boundaries and this alone changed my life so much. I started teaching other women about Narcissism and how to start their journey of healing. Together we worked on building our self-esteem, setting boundaries, dealing with past relationships and focusing more on self-care. This group grew so fast that I had to stop accepting new members, so that we could focus on the members who were already on the journey.

On this journey of healing, when you are speaking to people who have never encountered Narcissism, you will sound like a crazy person trying to explain it to them. You feel frustrated because they just don't get it. Although I was able to educate many people on the subject, I realized that it was time to refocus my energy back onto myself. I learned to talk to those who knew what I was going through and validated my experience and pain. You are never alone, even though it may feel like it. Don't isolate yourself, it is imperative that you don't do this in the healing process because being with a Narcissist is like having a drug addiction and many people end up right back in the abusive situation, so you don't want to try to do it alone.

Remember, the Narcissist will always find a way to hoover and get you back in the situation and under their mind control. They are so arrogant that it may even be through an email or a quick phone call. They love to drop bread crumbs to see if you are still weak for them. My Narcissist sent both of my daughters an Edible Arrangement on their birthdays. Nobody else knows what that means, but that was our special thing that we shared during our marriage. Whenever I was mad he would send me an Edible Arrangement.

They are very creative in their hoovering tactics to keep you thinking of them. My daughters would tell me how he would bribe them for personal information about my life, asking questions like where I work, do I have a boyfriend etc. He would also reach out and try to talk about sentimental moments that we shared, and how we could go back to those times. Once you respond, this tells them that they will always have a crack to get back into your life. After this type of interaction, you may not hear from them for a while because they are working on trapping their new supply source, since you have seen their mask fall and are no longer easy prey. They cannot survive without a main source of supply.

You will become their secondary supply source, so they can cause jealousy with the new supply (target).

Remember, you are dealing with master manipulators. That's why **No Contact** with them is ultimately the best way to deal with a Narcissist. That means no phone calls, text, emails, or social media interaction. You can't even sneak a peek at their Facebook page or Instagram. The reason behind this is that the Narcissist will use ANYTHING to get an emotional reaction from you. For example, they may post a picture with their new girlfriend, saying how happy they are. He may even check in and tag her on Facebook, at a restaurant you and him used frequent together. Only you and him will know the significance. He knows that if you see this, it will hurt you or bring up memories from your relationship. That's exactly what he wants. He will even take her on the same vacations he used to you take you on, and call her the same pet names he called you.

Yes, they are very clever with their tactics, but usually recycle them from relationship to relationship. Their ultimate goal is to make you suffer. They don't have to be even in your presence to get this twisted satisfaction. So, No Contact will save your life! If you have children together and you have to interact with them, the **Gray Rock** method is very useful, because they will not be able to get any emotion from you whether it be positive or negative.

Psychic Hoovering is another concept that many people who suffer from Narcissistic Abuse complain about. It sounds very foreign and even crazy to many, but I learned to understand it thoroughly by experience. You will think about them and they will suddenly call or email you at that moment. You are passing his favorite ice cream shop, and you get a message from him at that exact moment...Weird huh? You will start to think maybe you made a mistake and he is still your soul mate, because look, you are thinking about each other at the same time. You are on the same wavelength, right? Wrong! Once you have been through years and years of emotional manipulation and trauma with a Narcissist, you become connected to them energetically.

Religious people call it soul ties. You will still be able to feel their energy, even when they are no longer with you. This causes many survivors of Narcissistic Abuse to cycle in and out of depression and hopelessness for many years after leaving their relationship. People often ask, why can't you just get over it. They have no idea that the energy ties with a Narcissist will continue to connect you to negative emotions, people, places, and events, because that is what resonates with you. Many survivors will end up with another Narcissist right away, if they don't take the time to heal themselves.

Luckily, I discarded my Narcissist instead of the other way around, so it made my experience a little easier, since I had studied the disorder from front to back and inside out. I had to accept that I needed to move forward and that I may never get closure.

My ex still has never admitted to hitting me not one time. He told me that if it ever had happened it was my fault. He even went as far as telling his family and friends that he left me, and that I hurt him. During one of our exchanges for the children he asked me for a hug, and when he could tell that I was not interested, he told me he would never forgive me for the hurt I caused him throughout our relationship. I wish you could see my face as I am typing this. The nerve.

Conclusion

I had to know what I was dealing with if I was going to regain my freedom, and I did just that. I studied Narcissism from every angle. I wanted to know exactly what happened to me. My journey began to take on a new meaning. I wanted my life back, so I was going to do what I need to do to get it back. I realized that I needed to start surrounding myself with women who were once in my position, but who have overcome and are rebuilding their new foundation one brick at a time. I am not going to sugar coat this part of my journey at all, because I lost EVERYTHING.

The process was brutal, and painful. I was so angry, and what I felt like God was putting me through, when I had always been faithful to his word. The only thing I could do was hold on to God's promises of giving me back everything that I lost. I would fast and pray for his strength to move forward. My children who are already little empaths and prayer warriors, would pray every day for our success. Through this process, I learned a great lesson

He allowed the enemy to attack me, because he knew I would be tipped off to who I really am. I finally met Nisaa and Guess what?!?!?! She is beautiful, articulate, smart, dynamic, fierce, and the list goes on. She no longer needs anyone else to tell her who she is and to validate her existence. She is happily single and still not ready to mingle:). She used her struggle and pain to tap into what God created her to be.

Don't get me wrong, I still have a long way to go. I have even had my vulnerable moments with my ex-husband in the past, but I am no longer that woman or should I say the shell of that woman I was in my abusive relationship. I am genuinely happy with my new life and how far I have come. I challenge myself each day to live the life that God told me he had for me since I was a little girl. I challenge myself to do things that I used to fear. I no longer live in that imaginary box that kept me small and living a mediocre life... The infamous comfort zone. I AM FREE! I have become a successful business owner and a self-published author in the same year! God allowed me to rise from the ashes and I will forever be grateful! Thank you for taking the time to read my book.

I hope that it helped you to process your experience and know that life does go on. You do not have to stay stuck in a bad situation because you made a wrong choice. Life is full of wrong choices, which I refer to as "life lessons" or stepping stones to your greatness. If you trust the process and allow God to guide you towards your next steps, he will use all your perceived failures, to elevate you towards your purpose.

"It's ok if you fall down and lose your spark. Just make sure that when you get back up, you rise as the whole damn fire." – Colette Werden

Glossary of Terms

Adrenal Fatigue

Adrenal Fatigue is a stress-related condition that results in symptoms like exhaustion, weakened immunity, sleep disturbances, and food cravings.

Cognitive Dissonance

Cognitive Dissonance is the mental discomfort (psychological stress) experienced by a person who simultaneously holds two or more contradictory beliefs, ideas, or values.

Empath

An Empath is an individual that feels and absorb other people's emotions and/or physical symptoms because of their high sensitivities.

Flying Monkeys

Flying Monkeys are people who act on behalf of a narcissist to a third party, usually for an abusive purpose. They are usually unaware that they are being used.

Gaslighting

Gaslighting is used to manipulate (someone) by psychological means into questioning their own sanity.

Ghosting

Ghosting is the practice of ending a relationship with someone by suddenly and without explanation withdrawing from all communication.

Gray Rock

This method is where you become as exciting as a gray rock. You will respond with zero emotion to anything they do or say. This includes facial expressions and body language. You will make any communication with the Narcissist so boring, that they will get tired and look for another source of Narcissistic Supply.

Hoovering

Hoovering is a technique that is named after the Hoover vacuum cleaner and is used by Narcissists in order to "suck" their victims back into a relationship with them.

Idealize, Devalue, and Discard

The cycle that begins with a whirlwind romance, where the Narcissist will put you on a pedestal. Then before you know it they will start gaslighting, belittling you, and pulling disappearing acts, which will keep you off balance. Once the Devalue phase has been accomplished, you will be discarded as if you never existed and the silent treatment will begin. This can happen one time or over the years with a victim. They will just repeat the cycle throughout the relationship.

Love Bombing

Love bombing is an attempt to influence another person with over-the-top displays of attention and affection.

Narcissistic Injury

Narcissistic Injury A perceived threat to a narcissist's self-esteem or self-worth.

Narcissistic Pathological Envy

Pathological envy is a very intense and destructive emotion, born from deep emotional insecurities and poor sense of self-worth. When a target does something better than a Narcissist, it threatens their superiority and grandiose thoughts about themselves.

Narcissistic Smirk

The Narcissistic Smirk can usually be seen when you are in emotional or physical pain, usually of the narcissists making and they are exuding a weird glee that shines through their eyes.

Narcissistic Supply

Narcissistic Supply really refers to those people who provide a constant source of attention, approval, adoration, admiration, etc., for the narcissist.

No Contact

No contact is initiated as a way of breaking the emotional bonds between you and a narcissistic partner, friend or family member. This means no phone calls, text, emails, or social media contact. The only contact would be if you have children, and the interaction has to be void of emotion.

Post Traumatic Stress Disorder (PTSD)

A disorder that develops in some people who have experienced a shocking, scary, or dangerous event.

Projection

A projection is an unconscious defense mechanism in which the individual ejects aggressive, negative feelings and thoughts on to another person.

Psychic Hoovering

The method of Hoovering without being anywhere near the target using energy connections.

Silent Treatment

Silent Treatment is a tactic used by narcissists, to hold power and control in their relationships

Smear Campaign

An intense campaign designed to humiliate a victim to a person or group of people, while simultaneously elevating the narcissist.

Trauma Bonding

It's the type of bonding that can easily occur via passive-aggressive manipulation (i.e. sex, lies, silent treatments) and other manipulation tactics.

Triangulation

The act of a narcissist bringing in another person or group of people into the relationship to belittle the victim or make the victim vie for their attention. It can also be used as a way to draw you closer at the beginning of the relationship. The narcissist creates an aura of desirability, of being wanted by many, especially exes. They love to manufacture love triangle with exes.

About the Author

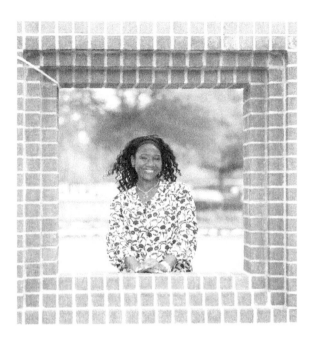

Nisaa Rahman Corbett, is the founder and owner of Keeping It Light, a company who has helped women from all over the globe, transform their lives and find their purpose. She is a certified Life Coach, who has led large groups of women in the fight to identify, escape, and recover from Narcissistic Abusive relationships. Nisaa graduated Summa Cum Laude from Houston Community College with an Associate's Degree in Criminal Justice. She also graduated Summa Cum Laude from the University of Houston-Downtown, where she obtained a B.S. Degree in Criminal Justice with a minor in Psychology. Nisaa is dedicated to leading women in the direction towards self-discovery, new beginnings and amazing transformations.

She was also featured as a Phenomenal Woman to Watch:
https://www.thesinglemomsguide.com/single-post/2018/03/07/Phenomenal-Woman-to-Watch-Nisaa-Corbett

Learn More About Narcissism

THIS IS A MUST READ:

https://blogs.psychcentral.com/relationships/2016/03/what-it-means-when-a-narcissist-says-i-love-you/

https://www.psychologytoday.com/blog/spycatcher/201709/how-narcissists-really-think

https://www.psychologytoday.com/blog/communication-success/201409/10-signs-youre-in-relationship-narcissist

https://narcissisticbehavior.net/narcissism-and-the-addiction-to-narcissistic-supply/

https://letmereach.com/2016/05/10/how-to-protect-yourself-against-psychic-hoovering/

https://thoughtcatalog.com/shahida-arabi/2017/05/3-powerful-ways-to-heal-from-the-toxic-triangulation-of-narcissists/

https://themindsjournal.com/psychic-hoovering/

Printed in Great Britain
by Amazon

54821090R00078